OLD MOORE'S

HOROSCOPE AND ASTRAL DIARY

SAGITTARIUS

OLD MOORE'S

HOROSCOPE AND ASTRAL DIARY

SAGITTARIUS

foulsham
LONDON • NEW YORK • TORONTO • SYDNEY

foulsham

The Publishing House, Bennetts Close,
Cippenham, Slough, Berks SL1 5AP, England

Foulsham books can be found in all good bookshops or direct from
www.foulsham.com

ISBN 978-0-572-03358-3

A CIP record for this book is available from the British Library

Printed in Great Britain by Cox & Wyman Ltd, Reading, Berkshire.

CONTENTS

INTRODUCTION

In the midst of our busy lives we often fail to take note of the subtle changes within our natures that take place on an almost moment-by-moment basis. Some of these are the natural result of circumstances that are brought to bear upon us but others are a direct response to the constantly changing patterns of the Sun, Moon and planets. Astrology gives us an opportunity to make the very best of what cosmological forces are acting upon us at any particular point in time, and Old Moore has been tracking planetary movements and the bearing they have on humanity for many centuries. The most recent result of these efforts is the Astral Diary for 2008 – a complete book geared specifically towards you and the influences that help to make you what you are.

If you want to know whether a new relationship is likely to turn out the way you hope, whether you are in for a good time in the financial stakes or if family pressures are likely to be making you less positive than you might usually be, Old Moore is the person to ask. The Astral Diary allows you an easy-to-follow, daily summing up of the way the stars and planets are affecting you and also tells you what you should be doing now in order to maximise your potential for the future. And there is also space in the diaries for your own comments and appointments.

Old Moore goes further than simply looking at your zodiac sign because unlike other yearly forecasts, the Astral Diaries allow you to look much deeper into your own individual nature. Your uniqueness is reflected by the time of day you were born and by the position of specific heavenly bodies, such as the Moon and the planet Venus. Using the Astral Diaries' unique tables you can work out what makes you tick in a much more personal sense. In possession of this information you can then deal much more effectively with the twists and turns of life and will know how to react to both good and not so favourable trends.

Every nuance of your nature is captured within your astrological profile and using the Astral Diary you can get so close to the core of planetary influence that you can almost feel the subtle undertones that, in the end, have a profound bearing on your life and circumstances. Used correctly, astrology allows you to maximise your potential, to strike whilst the iron is hot and to live a more contented and successful life. Consulting *Old Moore's Astral Diary* will make you more aware of what really makes you the person you are and is a fascinating way to register the very heartbeat of the solar system of which we are all a part.

Old Moore extends his customary greeting to all people of the Earth and offers his age-old wishes for a happy and prosperous period ahead.

THE ESSENCE OF SAGITTARIUS

Exploring the Personality of Sagittarius the Archer

(23RD NOVEMBER – 21ST DECEMBER)

What's in a sign?

Sagittarius is ruled by the large, expansive planet Jupiter, which from an astrological perspective makes all the difference to this happy-go-lucky and very enterprising zodiac sign. This is the sign of the Archer and there is a very good reason for our ancient ancestors having chosen the half-man, half-horse figure with its drawn bow. Not only are Sagittarians fleet-footed like a horse, but the remarks they make, like the arrow, go right to the target.

You love contentious situations and rarely shy away from controversy. With tremendous faith in your own abilities you are not easily kept down, and would usually find it relatively simple to persuade others to follow your course. Though you are born of a Fire sign, you are not as bullying as Aries can be, or as proud as a Leo. Despite this you do have a Fire-sign temper and can be a formidable opponent once you have your dander up.

You rarely choose to take the long route to any destination in life, preferring to drive forward as soon as your mind is made up. Communication comes easy to you and you add to your stock of weapons good intuitive insight and a capacity for brinkmanship that appears to know no bounds. At your best you are earnest, aspiring and honourable, though on the other side of the coin Sagittarians can make the best con artists of all!

What you hate most is to be discouraged, or for others to thwart your intentions. There is a slight tendency for you to use others whilst you are engaging in many of the schemes that are an intrinsic part of your life, though you would never deliberately hurt or offend anyone.

Sagittarian people are natural lovers of fun. When what is required is a shot of enthusiasm, or an immediacy that can cut right through the middle of any red tape, it is the Archer who invariably ends up in charge. When others panic, you come into your own, and you have an ability to get things done in a quarter of the expected time. Whether they are completed perfectly, however, is a different matter altogether.

Sagittarius resources

Sagittarians appear to be the natural conjurors of the zodiac. The stage magician seems to draw objects from thin air, and it often appears that the Archer is able to do something similar. This is an intriguing process to observe, but somewhat difficult to explain. Sagittarians seem to be able to get directly to the heart of any matter, and find it easy to circumnavigate potential difficulties. Thus they achieve objectives that look impossible to observers – hence the conjuring analogy.

Just as the biblical David managed to defeat Goliath with nothing more than a humble pebble and a sling, Sagittarius also goes seemingly naked into battle. The Archer relies on his or her natural wit, together with a fairly instinctive intelligence, a good deal of common sense and a silver tongue. The patient observer must inevitably come to the conclusion that what really matters isn't what the Sagittarian can do, but how much they manage to get others to undertake on their behalf. In other words, people follow your lead without question. This quality can be one of your best resources and only fails when you have doubt about yourself, which fortunately is very rarely.

If other signs could sell refrigerators to Eskimos, you could add a deep-freeze complete with ice tray! This is one of the reasons why so many Archers are engaged in both advertising and marketing. Not only do you know what people want, you also have an instinctive ability to make them want whatever it is you have on offer.

It is likely that you would see nothing remotely mysterious about your ability to peer through to the heart of any matter. In the main you would refer to this as 'gut reaction', despite the fact that it looks distinctly magical to those around you. Fortunately this is part of your mystique, and even if you should choose to take someone for a complete ride, it is doubtful that they would end up disliking you as a result. You don't set out to be considered a genius, and you manage to retain the common touch. This is extremely important, for those with whom you have contacts actively want to help you because you are a 'regular guy'.

Beneath the surface

People tend to be very complicated. Untangling their motives in any given situation is rarely easy. Psychologists have many theories regarding the working of the human psyche and philosophers have struggled with such matters for thousands of years. Clearly none of these people were looking at the zodiac sign of Sagittarius. Ask the average Archer why they did this or that thing and the chances are that you will get a reply something very similar to 'Well, it seemed like a good idea at the time'.

While many people might claim to be uncomplicated, at heart you genuinely are. Complications are something you try to avoid, even though some of your deals in life might look like a roll of barbed wire to those around you. In the main you keep your objectives as simple as possible. This is one of the reasons why it isn't particularly difficult for you to circumnavigate some of the potential pitfalls – you simply won't recognise that they exist. Setting your eyes on the horizon you set off with a jaunty step, refusing to acknowledge problems and, when necessary, sorting them out on the way.

Your general intention is to succeed and this fact permeates just about every facet of your life. Satisfaction doesn't necessarily come for you from a job well done, because the word 'well' in this context often isn't especially important. And when you have one task out of the way, you immediately set your sights on something else. Trying to figure out exactly why you live your life in the way you do, your psychological imperatives and ultimate intentions, costs you too much time, so you probably don't indulge in such idle speculation at all.

You have a warm heart and always want the best for everyone. It almost never occurs to you that other people don't think about things in the way you might and you automatically assume that others will be only too pleased to follow your lead. In the main you are uncomplicated, don't indulge in too many frills and fancies and speak your mind. There really isn't much difference between what you do in life, and what you think about your actions. This is not to infer that you are shallow, merely that you don't see much point in complicating the obvious with too much internal musing.

One of the main reasons why people like you so much is because the 'what you see is what you get' adage is more true in your case than in any other.

Making the best of yourself

Always on the go and invariably looking for a new challenge, it isn't hard to see how Sagittarius makes the best of itself. This is a dynamic, thrusting sign, with a thirst for adventure and a great ability to think on its feet. As a child of Sagittarius you need the cut and thrust of an exciting life in order to show your true mettle. It doesn't do for you to sit around inactive for any length of time and any sort of enforced lay-off is likely to drive you to distraction.

In a career situation your natural proclivities show through, so it's best for you to be in some position which necessitates decision making on a moment-by-moment basis. Production-line work or tasks that involve going over the same ground time and again are not really your forte, though you are certainly not afraid of hard work and can labour on regardless towards any objective – just as long as there is a degree of excitement on the way.

Socially speaking you probably have many friends, and that's the way you like things to be. You need to know that people rate you highly, and will usually be on hand to offer the sort of advice that is always interesting, but probably not totally reasoned. It's a fact that you think everyone has the same ability to think on their feet that typifies your nature, and you trust everyone instinctively – at least once.

In love you need the sort of relationship that allows a degree of personal freedom. You can't be fettered and so have to be your own person under all situations. You are kind and attentive, though sometimes get carried away with the next grand scheme and so you need an understanding partner. Archers should not tie themselves down too early in life and are at their best surrounded by those who love the dynamism and difficult-to-predict qualities exemplified by this zodiac sign.

Most important of all you need to be happy with your lot. Living through restricted or miserable times takes its toll. Fortunately these are few in your life, mainly because of the effort you put into life yourself.

The impressions you give

You must be doing something right because it's a fact that Sagittarius represents one of the most instinctively liked zodiac signs. There are many reasons for this state of affairs. For starters you will always do others a good turn if it's possible. It's true that you are a bit of a rogue on occasions, but that only endears you to the sort of individuals with whom you choose to share your life. You are always the first with a joke, even under difficult circumstances, and you face problems with an open mind and a determination to get through them. On the way you acquire many friends, though in your case many 'acquaintances' might be nearer the mark. This is a situation of your own choosing and though you have so much to recommend you to others, it's a fact that you keep really close ties to the absolute minimum.

Some people might think you rather superficial and perhaps an intellectual lightweight. If so, this only comes about because they don't understand the way your mind works. All the same it is your own nature that leads a few individuals to these conclusions. You can skip from one subject to another, are an insatiable flirt in social situations and love to tell funny stories. 'Depth' isn't really your thing and that means that you could appear to lower the tone of conversations that are getting too heavy for your liking. You do need to be the centre of attention most of the time, which won't exactly endear you to others who have a similar disposition.

People know that you have a temper, like all Fire signs. They will also realise that your outbursts are rare, short-lived and of no real note. You don't bear a grudge and quickly learn that friends are more useful than enemies under any circumstance.

You come across as the capricious, bubbly, lively, likeable child of the zodiac and under such circumstances it would be very difficult for anyone to find fault with you for long. Often outrageous, always interesting and seldom down in the dumps – it's hard to see how you could fail to be loved.

The way forward

It might be best to realise, right from the outset, that you are not indestructible. Deep inside you have all the same insecurities, vulnerabilities and paranoia that the rest of humanity possesses. As a Sagittarian it doesn't do to dwell on such matters, but at least the acknowledgement might stop you going over the edge sometimes. You come from a part of the zodiac that has to be active and which must show itself in the best possible light all the time, and that's a process that is very demanding.

In the main, however, you relish the cut and thrust of life and it is quite likely that you already have the necessary recipe for happiness and success. If you don't, then you are involved in a search that is likely to be both interesting and rewarding, because it isn't really the objective that matters to you but rather the fun you can have on the way.

Be as honest as you can with those around you, though without losing that slightly roguish charm that makes you so appealing. At the same time try to ensure that your own objectives bear others in mind. You can sometimes be a little fickle and, in rare circumstances, unscrupulous. At heart though, you have your own moral convictions and would rarely do anyone a bad turn. On the contrary, you do your best to help those around you, and invariably gain in popularity on the way.

Health-wise you are probably fairly robust but you can run your nervous system into the ground on occasions. There are times when a definite routine suits you physically, but this doesn't always agree with your mental make-up, which is essentially driving and demanding. The peaks and troughs of your life are an inevitable part of what makes you tick, and you would be a poorer person without them.

Explaining yourself is not generally difficult, and neither is the search for personal success, even if you keep looking beyond it to even greater achievements further down the road. Being loved is important, despite the fact that you would deny this on occasions. Perhaps you don't always know yourself as well as you might, though since you are not an inveterate deep thinker it is likely that this is not a problem to you.

If you are already an adult, it's likely the path you are presently following is the one for you. That doesn't mean to say that you will keep to it, or find it universally rewarding. You find new promise in each day, and that's the joy of Sagittarius.

SAGITTARIUS ON THE CUSP

Old Moore is often asked how astrological profiles are altered for those people born at either the beginning or the end of a zodiac sign, or, more properly, on the cusps of a sign. In the case of Sagittarius this would be on the 23rd of November and for two or three days after, and similarly at the end of the sign, probably from the 19th to the 21st of December. In this year's Astral Diaries, once again, Old Moore sets out to explain the differences regarding cuspid signs.

The Scorpio Cusp – November 23rd to 25th

You could turn out to be one of the most well-liked people around, especially if you draw heavily from the more positive qualities of the two zodiac signs that have the most profound part to play in your life. Taken alone the Sagittarian is often accused of being rather too flighty. Sagittarians are often guilty of flirting and sometimes fall foul of people who take a more serious view of life in general. The presence in your make-up of the much deeper and more contemplative sign of Scorpio brings a quiet and a sense of reserve that the Sagittarian nature sometimes lacks. Although you like to have a good time and would be more than willing to dance the night away, you are probably also happy enough when the time comes to go home. Family means much to you and you have a great sensitivity to the needs of those around you. What makes all the difference is that you not only understand others, but you have the potential to take practical steps to help them.

You are probably not quite the workaholic that the Archer alone tends to be and can gain rest and relaxation, which has to be good for you in the longer term. You don't lack the ability to be successful but your level of application is considered, less frenetic and altogether more ordered. It's true that some confusion comes into your life from time to time, but you have the resources to deal with such eventualities, and you do so with a smile on your face most of the time. People would warm to you almost instantly and you are likely to do whatever you can to support family members and friends.

Often sinking into a dream world if you feel threatened, some of the achievements that are second nature to the Sagittarian are left on the shelf for a while. There are times when this turns out to be a blessing, if only because your actions are more considered. Personality clashes with others are less likely with this combination and Sagittarius also modifies the slightly moody qualities that come with Scorpio alone. More methodical in every way than the usual Archer, in many situations you are a good combination of optimist and pessimist.

The Capricorn Cusp – December 19th to 21st

The fact that comes across almost immediately with the Capricorn cusp of Sagittarius is how very practical you tend to be. Most of you would be ideal company on a desert island, for a number of reasons. Firstly you are quite self-contained, which Sagittarius taken alone certainly is not. You would soon get your head round the practical difficulties of finding food and shelter, and would be very happy to provide these necessities for your companions too. Unlike the typical Sagittarian you do not boast and probably do not come across as being quite so overbearing as the Archer seems to be. For all this you are friendly, chatty, love to meet many different and interesting types and do whatever you can to be of assistance to a world which is all the better for having you in it.

There is less of a tendency for you to worry at a superficial level than Sagittarius alone is inclined to do, mainly because long periods of practical application bring with them a contemplative tendency that Sagittarius sometimes lacks. In love you tend to be quite sincere, even if the slightly fickle tendencies of the Archer do show through now and again. Any jealousy that is levelled at you by your partner could be as a result of your natural attractiveness, which you probably don't seek. Fairly comfortable in almost any sort of company, you are at your best when faced with individuals who have something intelligent and interesting to say. As a salesperson you would be second to none, but it would be essential for you to believe absolutely in the product or service you were selling.

Almost any sort of work is possible in your case, though you wouldn't take too kindly to being restricted in any way, and need the chance to show what your practical nature is worth, as well as your keen perception and organisational abilities. What matters most for you at work is that you are well liked by others and that you manage to maintain a position of control through inspiring confidence. On a creative level, the combination of Sagittarius and Capricorn would make you a good sculptor, or possibly a natural landscape gardener.

SAGITTARIUS AND ITS ASCENDANTS

The nature of every individual on the planet is composed of the rich variety of zodiac signs and planetary positions that were present at the time of their birth. Your Sun sign, which in your case is Sagittarius, is one of the many factors when it comes to assessing the unique person you are. Probably the most important consideration, other than your Sun sign, is to establish the zodiac sign that was rising over the eastern horizon at the time that you were born. This is your Ascending or Rising sign. Most popular astrology fails to take account of the Ascendant, and yet its importance remains with you from the very moment of your birth, through every day of your life. The Ascendant is evident in the way you approach the world, and so, when meeting a person for the first time, it is this astrological influence that you are most likely to notice first. Our Ascending sign essentially represents what we appear to be, while the Sun sign is what we feel inside ourselves.

The Ascendant also has the potential for modifying our overall nature. For example, if you were born at a time of day when Sagittarius was passing over the eastern horizon (this would be around the time of dawn) then you would be classed as a double Sagittarius. As such, you would typify this zodiac sign, both internally and in your dealings with others. However, if your Ascendant sign turned out to be an Earth sign, such as Taurus, there would be a profound alteration of nature, away from the expected qualities of Sagittarius.

One of the reasons why popular astrology often ignores the Ascendant is that it has always been rather difficult to establish. Old Moore has found a way to make this possible by devising an easy-to-use table, which you will find on page 158 of this book. Using this, you can establish your Ascendant sign at a glance. You will need to know your rough time of birth, then it is simply a case of following the instructions.

For those readers who have no idea of their time of birth it might be worth allowing a good friend, or perhaps your partner, to read through the section that follows this introduction. Someone who deals with you on a regular basis may easily discover your Ascending sign, even though you could have some difficulty establishing it for yourself. A good understanding of this component of your nature is essential if you want to be aware of that 'other person' who is responsible for the way you make contact with the world at large. Your Sun sign, Ascendant sign, and the other pointers in this book will, together, allow you a far better understanding of what makes you tick as an individual. Peeling back the different layers of your astrological make-up can be an enlightening experience, and the Ascendant may represent one of the most important layers of all.

Sagittarius with Sagittarius Ascendant

You are very easy to spot, even in a crowd. There is hardly a more dynamic individual to be found anywhere in the length and breadth of the zodiac. You know what you want from life and have a pretty good idea about how you will get it. The fact that you are always so cocksure is a source of great wonder to those around you, but they can't see deep inside, where you are not half as certain as you appear to be. In the main you show yourself to be kind, attentive, caring and a loyal friend. To balance this, you are determined and won't be thwarted by anything.

You keep up a searing pace through life and sometimes find it difficult to understand those people who have slightly less energy. In your better moments you understand that you are unique and will wait for others to catch up. Quite often you need periods of rest in order to recharge batteries that run down through over-use, but it doesn't take you too long to get yourself back on top form. In matters of the heart you can be slightly capricious, but you are a confident lover who knows the right words and gestures. If you are ever accused of taking others for granted you might need to indulge in some self-analysis.

Sagittarius with Capricorn Ascendant

The typical Sagittarian nature is modified for the better when Capricorn is part of the deal. It's true that you manage to push forward progressively under most circumstances, but you also possess staying power and can work long and hard to achieve your objectives, most of which are carefully planned in advance. Few people have the true measure of your nature, for it runs rather deeper than appears to be the case on the surface. Routines don't bother you as much as would be the case for Sagittarius when taken alone, and you don't care if any objective takes weeks, months or even years to achieve. You are very fond of those you take to, and prove to be a capable friend, even when things get tough.

In love relationships you are steadfast and reliable, and yet you never lose the ability to entertain. Yours is a dry sense of humour which shows itself to a multitude of different people and which doesn't evaporate, even on those occasions when life gets tough. It might take you a long time to find the love of your life, but when you do there is a greater possibility of retaining the relationship for a long period. You don't tend to inherit money, but you can easily make it for yourself, though you don't worry too much about the amount. On the whole you are self-sufficient and sensible.

Sagittarius with Aquarius Ascendant

There is an original streak to your nature which is very attractive to the people with whom you share your life. Always different, ever on the go and anxious to try out the next experiment in life, you are interested in almost everything and yet deeply attached to almost nothing. Everyone you know thinks that you are a little 'odd', but you probably don't mind them believing this because you know it to be true. In fact it is possible that you positively relish your eccentricity, which sets you apart from the common herd and means that you are always going to be noticed.

Although it may seem strange with this combination of Air and Fire, you can be distinctly cool on occasions, have a deep and abiding love of your own company now and again, and won't easily be understood. Love comes fairly easily to you but there are times when you are accused of being self-possessed, self-indulgent and not willing enough to fall in line with the wishes of those around you. Despite this you walk on and on down your own path. At heart you are an extrovert and you love to party, often late into the night. Luxury appeals to you, though it tends to be of the transient sort. Travel could easily play a major and a very important part in your life.

Sagittarius with Pisces Ascendant

A very attractive combination this, because the more dominant qualities of the Archer are somehow mellowed-out by the caring Water-sign qualities of the Fishes. You can be very outgoing, but there is always a deeper side to your nature that allows others to know that you are thinking about them. Few people could fall out with either your basic nature or your attitude to the world at large, even though there are depths to your personality that may not be easily understood. You are capable, have a good executive ability and can work hard to achieve your objectives, even if you get a little disillusioned on the way. Much of your life is given over to helping those around you and there is a great tendency for you to work for and on behalf of humanity as a whole. A sense of community is brought to most of what you do and you enjoy co-operation.

Although you have the natural Sagittarian ability to attract people to you, the Pisces half of your nature makes you just a little more reserved in personal matters than might otherwise be the case. More careful in your choices than either sign taken alone, you still have to make certain that your motivations when commencing a personal relationship are the right ones. You love to be happy, and to offer gifts of happiness to others.

Sagittarius with Aries Ascendant

What a lovely combination this can be, for the devil-may-care aspects of Sagittarius lighten the load of a sometimes too serious Aries interior. Everything that glistens is not gold, though it's hard to convince you of the fact because, to mix metaphors, you can make a silk purse out of a sow's ear. Almost everyone loves you, and in return you offer a friendship that is warm and protective, but not as demanding as sometimes tends to be the case with the Aries type. Relationships may be many and varied and there is often more than one major attachment in the life of those holding this combination. You can bring a breath of spring to any relationship, though you need to ensure that the person concerned is capable of keeping up with the hectic pace of your life.

It may appear from time to time that you are rather too trusting for your own good, though deep inside you are very astute, and it seems that almost everything you undertake works out well in the end. This has nothing to do with native luck and is really down to the fact that you are much more calculating than might appear to be the case at first sight. As a parent you are protective, yet offer sufficient room for self-expression.

Sagittarius with Taurus Ascendant

A dual nature is evident here, and if it doesn't serve to confuse you it will certainly be a cause of concern to many of the people with whom you share your life. You like to have a good time and are a natural party-goer. On such occasions you are accommodating, chatty and good to know. But contrast this with the quieter side of Taurus, which is directly opposed to your Sagittarian qualities. The opposition of forces is easy for you to deal with because you inhabit your own body and mind all the time, but it's far less easy for friends and relatives to understand. As a result, on those occasions when you decide that, socially speaking, enough is enough, you will need to explain the fact to the twelve people who are waiting outside your door with party hats and whoopee cushions.

Confidence to do almost anything is not far from the forefront of your mind and you readily embark on adventures that would have some types flapping about in horror. Here again, it is important to realise that we are not all built the same way and that gentle coaxing is sometimes necessary to bring others round to your point of view. If you really have a fault, it could be that you are so busy being your own, rather less than predictable self, that you fail to take the rest of the world into account.

17

Sagittarius with Gemini Ascendant

'Tomorrow is another day!' This is your belief and you stick to it. There isn't a brighter and more optimistic soul to be found than you and almost everyone you come into contact with is touched by the fact. Dashing about from one place to another, you manage to get more things done in one day than most other people would achieve in a week. Of course this explains why you are so likely to wear yourself out and it means that frequent periods of absolute rest are necessary if you are to remain truly healthy and happy. Sagittarius makes you brave and sometimes a little headstrong, so you need to curb your natural enthusiasm while you stop to think about the consequences of your actions.

It's not really certain if you do 'think' in the accepted sense of the word, because the lightning qualities of both these signs mean that your reactions are second to none. However, you are not indestructible and you put far more pressure on yourself than would often be sensible. Routines are not your thing at all, and many of you manage to hold down two or more jobs at once. It might be an idea to stop and smell the flowers on the way, and you could certainly do with putting your feet up much more than you do. However, you probably won't still be reading this passage because you will have something far more important to do!

Sagittarius with Cancer Ascendant

You have far more drive, enthusiasm and get-up-and-go than would seem to be the case for Cancer when taken alone, but all of this is tempered with a certain quiet compassion that probably makes you the best sort of Sagittarian too. It's true that you don't like to be on your own or to retire in your shell quite as much as the Crab usually does, though there are, even in your case, occasions when this is going to be necessary. Absolute concentration can sometimes be a problem to you, though this is hardly likely to be the case when you are dealing with matters relating to your home or family, both of which reign supreme in your thinking. Always loving and kind, you are a social animal and enjoy being out there in the real world, expressing the deeper opinions of Cancer much more readily than would often be the case with other combinations relating to the sign of the Crab.

Personality is not lacking and you tend to be very popular, not least because you are the fountain of good and practical advice. You want to get things done and retain a practical approach to most situations which is the envy of many other people. As a parent you are second to none, combining common sense, dignity and a sensible approach. To balance this you stay young enough to understand children.

Sagittarius with Leo Ascendant

Above and beyond anything else you are naturally funny, and this is an aspect of your nature that will bring you intact through a whole series of problems that you manage to create for yourself. Chatty, witty, charming, kind and loving, you personify the best qualities of both these signs, whilst also retaining the Fire-sign ability to keep going, long after the rest of the party has gone home to bed. Being great fun to have around, you attract friends in the way that a magnet attracts iron filings. Many of these will be casual connections but there will always be a nucleus of deep, abiding attachments that may stay around you for most of your life.

You don't often suffer from fatigue, but on those occasions when you do there is ample reason to stay still for a while and to take stock of situations. Routines are not your thing and you like to fill your life with variety. It's important to do certain things right, however, and staying power is something that comes with age, assisted by the Fixed quality of Leo. Few would lock horns with you in an argument, which you always have to win. In a way you are a natural debator but you can sometimes carry things too far if you are up against a worthy opponent. You have the confidence to sail through situations that would defeat others.

Sagittarius with Virgo Ascendant

This is a combination that might look rather odd at first sight because these two signs have so very little in common. However, the saying goes that opposites attract, and in terms of the personality you display to the world this is especially true in your case. Not everyone understands what makes you tick but you try to show the least complicated face to the world that you can manage to display. You can be deep and secretive on occasions, and yet at other times you can start talking as soon as you climb out of bed and never stop until you are back there again. Inspirational and spontaneous, you take the world by storm on those occasions when you are free from worries and firing on all cylinders. It is a fact that you support your friends, though there are rather more of them than would be the case for Virgo taken on its own, and you don't always choose them as wisely as you might.

There are times when you display a temper, and although Sagittarius is incapable of bearing a grudge, the same cannot be said for Virgo, which has a better memory than the elephant. For the best results in life you need to relax as much as possible and avoid overheating that powerful and busy brain. Virgo gives you the ability to concentrate on one thing at once, a skill you should encourage.

19

Sagittarius with Libra Ascendant

A very happy combination this, with a great desire for life in all its forms and a need to push forward the bounds of the possible in a way that few other zodiac sign connections would do. You don't like the unpleasant or ugly in life and yet you are capable of dealing with both if you have to. Giving so much to humanity, you still manage to retain a degree of individuality that would surprise many, charm others, and please all.

On the reverse side of the same coin you might find that you are sometimes accused of being fickle, but this is only an expression of your need for change and variety, which is intrinsic to both these signs. True, you have more of a temper than would be the case for Libra when taken on its own, but such incidents would see you up and down in a flash and it is almost impossible for you to bear a grudge of any sort. Routines get on your nerves and you are far happier when you can please yourself and get ahead at your own pace, which is quite fast.

As a lover you can make a big impression and most of you will not go short of affection in the early days, before you choose to commit yourself. Once you do, there is always a chance of romantic problems, but these are less likely when you have chosen carefully in the first place.

Sagittarius with Scorpio Ascendant

There are many gains with this combination, and most of you reading this will already be familiar with the majority of them. Sagittarius offers a bright and hopeful approach to life, but may not always have the staying power and the patience to get what it really needs. Scorpio, on the other hand, can be too deep for its own good, is very self-seeking on occasions and extremely giving to others. Both the signs have problems when taken on their own, and, it has to be said, double the difficulties when they come together. But this is not usually the case. Invariably the presence of Scorpio slows down the over-quick responses of the Archer, whilst the inclusion of Sagittarius prevents Scorpio from taking itself too seriously.

Life is so often a game of extremes, when all the great spiritual masters of humanity have indicated that a 'middle way' is the path to choose. You have just the right combination of skills and mental faculties to find that elusive path, and can bring great joy to yourself and others as a result. Most of the time you are happy, optimistic, helpful and a joy to know. You have mental agility, backed up by a stunning intuition, which itself would rarely let you down. Keep a sense of proportion and understand that your depth of intellect is necessary in order to curb the more flighty aspects of Scorpio.

THE MOON AND THE PART IT PLAYS IN YOUR LIFE

In astrology the Moon is probably the single most important heavenly body after the Sun. Its unique position, as partner to the Earth on its journey around the solar system, means that the Moon appears to pass through the signs of the zodiac extremely quickly. The zodiac position of the Moon at the time of your birth plays a great part in personal character and is especially significant in the build-up of your emotional nature.

Sun Moon Cycles

The first lunar cycle deals with the part the position of the Moon plays relative to your Sun sign. I have made the fluctuations of this pattern easy for you to understand by means of a simple cyclic graph. It appears on the first page of each 'Your Month At A Glance', under the title 'Highs and Lows'. The graph displays the lunar cycle and you will soon learn to understand how its movements have a bearing on your level of energy and your abilities.

Your Own Moon Sign

Discovering the position of the Moon at the time of your birth has always been notoriously difficult because tracking the complex zodiac positions of the Moon is not easy. This process has been reduced to three simple stages with Old Moore's unique Lunar Tables. A breakdown of the Moon's zodiac positions can be found from page 25 onwards, so that once you know what your Moon Sign is, you can see what part this plays in the overall build-up of your personal character.

If you follow the instructions on the next page you will soon be able to work out exactly what zodiac sign the Moon occupied on the day that you were born and you can then go on to compare the reading for this position with those of your Sun sign and your Ascendant. It is partly the comparison between these three important positions that goes towards making you the unique individual you are.

HOW TO DISCOVER YOUR MOON SIGN

This is a three-stage process. You may need a pen and a piece of paper but if you follow the instructions below the process should only take a minute or so.

STAGE 1 First of all you need to know the Moon Age at the time of your birth. If you look at Moon Table 1, on page 23, you will find all the years between 1910 and 2008 down the left side. Find the year of your birth and then trace across to the right to the month of your birth. Where the two intersect you will find a number. This is the date of the New Moon in the month that you were born. You now need to count forward the number of days between the New Moon and your own birthday. For example, if the New Moon in the month of your birth was shown as being the 6th and you were born on the 20th, your Moon Age Day would be 14. If the New Moon in the month of your birth came after your birthday, you need to count forward from the New Moon in the previous month. Whatever the result, jot this number down so that you do not forget it.

STAGE 2 Take a look at Moon Table 2 on page 24. Down the left hand column look for the date of your birth. Now trace across to the month of your birth. Where the two meet you will find a letter. Copy this letter down alongside your Moon Age Day.

STAGE 3 Moon Table 3 on page 24 will supply you with the zodiac sign the Moon occupied on the day of your birth. Look for your Moon Age Day down the left hand column and then for the letter you found in Stage 2. Where the two converge you will find a zodiac sign and this is the sign occupied by the Moon on the day that you were born.

Your Zodiac Moon Sign Explained

You will find a profile of all zodiac Moon Signs on pages 25 to 28, showing in yet another way how astrology helps to make you into the individual that you are. In each daily entry of the Astral Diary you can find the zodiac position of the Moon for every day of the year. This also allows you to discover your lunar birthdays. Since the Moon passes through all the signs of the zodiac in about a month, you can expect something like twelve lunar birthdays each year. At these times you are likely to be emotionally steady and able to make the sort of decisions that have real, lasting value.

MOON TABLE 1

YEAR	OCT	NOV	DEC	YEAR	OCT	NOV	DEC	YEAR	OCT	NOV	DEC
1910	2	1	1/30	1943	29	27	27	1976	23	21	21
1911	21	20	20	1944	17	15	15	1977	12	11	10
1912	11	9	9	1945	6	4	4	1978	2/31	30	29
1913	29	28	27	1946	24	23	23	1979	20	19	18
1914	19	17	17	1947	14	12	12	1980	9	8	7
1915	8	7	6	1948	2	1	1/30	1981	27	26	26
1916	27	26	25	1949	21	20	19	1982	17	15	15
1917	15	14	13	1950	11	9	9	1983	6	4	4
1918	4	3	2	1951	1/30	29	28	1984	24	22	22
1919	23	22	21	1952	18	17	17	1985	14	12	12
1920	12	10	10	1953	8	6	6	1986	3	2	1/30
1921	1/30	29	29	1954	26	25	25	1987	22	21	20
1922	20	19	18	1955	15	14	14	1988	10	9	9
1923	10	8	8	1956	4	2	2	1989	29	28	28
1924	28	26	26	1957	23	21	21	1990	18	17	17
1925	17	16	15	1958	12	11	10	1991	8	6	6
1926	6	5	5	1959	2/31	30	29	1992	25	24	24
1927	25	24	24	1960	20	19	18	1993	15	14	14
1928	14	12	12	1961	9	8	7	1994	5	3	2
1929	2	1	1/30	1962	28	27	26	1995	24	22	22
1930	20	19	19	1963	17	15	15	1996	11	10	10
1931	11	9	9	1964	5	4	4	1997	31	30	29
1932	29	27	27	1965	24	22	22	1998	20	19	18
1933	19	17	17	1966	14	12	12	1999	8	8	7
1934	8	7	6	1967	3	2	1/30	2000	27	26	25
1935	27	26	25	1968	22	21	20	2001	17	16	15
1936	15	14	13	1969	10	9	9	2002	6	4	4
1937	4	3	2	1970	1/30	29	28	2003	25	24	23
1938	23	22	21	1971	19	18	17	2004	12	11	11
1939	12	11	10	1972	8	6	6	2005	2	1	1/31
1940	1/30	29	28	1973	26	25	25	2006	21	20	20
1941	20	19	18	1974	15	14	14	2007	11	9	9
1942	10	8	8	1975	5	3	3	2008	29	28	27

TABLE 2

DAY	NOV	DEC
1	e	i
2	e	i
3	e	m
4	f	m
5	f	n
6	f	n
7	f	n
8	f	n
9	f	n
10	f	n
11	f	n
12	f	n
13	g	n
14	g	n
15	g	n
16	g	n
17	g	n
18	g	n
19	g	n
20	g	n
21	g	n
22	g	n
23	i	q
24	i	q
25	i	q
26	i	q
27	i	q
28	i	q
29	i	q
30	i	q
31	–	q

MOON TABLE 3

M/D	e	f	g	i	m	n	q
0	SC	SC	SC	SA	SA	SA	CP
1	SC	SC	SA	SA	SA	CP	CP
2	SC	SA	SA	CP	CP	CP	AQ
3	SA	SA	CP	CP	CP	AQ	AQ
4	SA	CP	CP	CP	AQ	AQ	PI
5	CP	CP	AQ	AQ	AQ	PI	PI
6	CP	AQ	AQ	AQ	AQ	PI	AR
7	AQ	AQ	PI	PI	PI	AR	AR
8	AQ	PI	PI	PI	PI	AR	AR
9	AQ	PI	PI	AR	AR	TA	TA
10	PI	AR	AR	AR	AR	TA	TA
11	PI	AR	AR	TA	TA	TA	GE
12	AR	TA	TA	TA	TA	GE	GE
13	AR	TA	TA	GE	GE	GE	GE
14	TA	GE	GE	GE	GE	CA	CA
15	TA	TA	TA	GE	GE	GE	CA
16	TA	GE	GE	GE	CA	CA	CA
17	GE	GE	GE	CA	CA	CA	LE
18	GE	GE	CA	CA	CA	LE	LE
19	GE	CA	CA	CA	LE	LE	LE
20	CA	CA	CA	LE	LE	LE	VI
21	CA	CA	LE	LE	LE	VI	VI
22	CA	LE	LE	VI	VI	VI	LI
23	LE	LE	LE	VI	VI	VI	LI
24	LE	LE	VI	VI	VI	LI	LI
25	LE	VI	VI	LI	LI	LI	SC
26	VI	VI	LI	LI	LI	SC	SC
27	VI	LI	LI	SC	SC	SC	SA
28	LI	LI	LI	SC	SC	SC	SA
29	LI	LI	SC	SC	SA	SA	SA

AR = Aries, TA = Taurus, GE = Gemini, CA = Cancer, LE = Leo, VI = Virgo, LI = Libra, SC = Scorpio, SA = Sagittarius, CP = Capricorn, AQ = Aquarius, PI = Pisces

MOON SIGNS

Moon in Aries

You have a strong imagination, courage, determination and a desire to do things in your own way and forge your own path through life.

Originality is a key attribute; you are seldom stuck for ideas although your mind is changeable and you could take the time to focus on individual tasks. Often quick-tempered, you take orders from few people and live life at a fast pace. Avoid health problems by taking regular time out for rest and relaxation.

Emotionally, it is important that you talk to those you are closest to and work out your true feelings. Once you discover that people are there to help, there is less necessity for you to do everything yourself.

Moon in Taurus

The Moon in Taurus gives you a courteous and friendly manner, which means you are likely to have many friends.

The good things in life mean a lot to you, as Taurus is an Earth sign that delights in experiences which please the senses. Hence you are probably a lover of good food and drink, which may in turn mean you need to keep an eye on the bathroom scales, especially as looking good is also important to you.

Emotionally you are fairly stable and you stick by your own standards. Taureans do not respond well to change. Intuition also plays an important part in your life.

Moon in Gemini

You have a warm-hearted character, sympathetic and eager to help others. At times reserved, you can also be articulate and chatty: this is part of the paradox of Gemini, which always brings duplicity to the nature. You are interested in current affairs, have a good intellect, and are good company and likely to have many friends. Most of your friends have a high opinion of you and would be ready to defend you should the need arise. However, this is usually unnecessary, as you are quite capable of defending yourself in any verbal confrontation.

Travel is important to your inquisitive mind and you find intellectual stimulus in mixing with people from different cultures. You also gain much from reading, writing and the arts but you do need plenty of rest and relaxation in order to avoid fatigue.

Moon in Cancer

The Moon in Cancer at the time of birth is a fortunate position as Cancer is the Moon's natural home. This means that the qualities of compassion and understanding given by the Moon are especially enhanced in your nature, and you are friendly and sociable and cope well with emotional pressures. You cherish home and family life, and happily do the domestic tasks. Your surroundings are important to you and you hate squalor and filth. You are likely to have a love of music and poetry.

Your basic character, although at times changeable like the Moon itself, depends on symmetry. You aim to make your surroundings comfortable and harmonious, for yourself and those close to you.

Moon in Leo

The best qualities of the Moon and Leo come together to make you warm-hearted, fair, ambitious and self-confident. With good organisational abilities, you invariably rise to a position of responsibility in your chosen career. This is fortunate as you don't enjoy being an 'also-ran' and would rather be an important part of a small organisation than a menial in a large one.

You should be lucky in love, and happy, provided you put in the effort to make a comfortable home for yourself and those close to you. It is likely that you will have a love of pleasure, sport, music and literature. Life brings you many rewards, most of them as a direct result of your own efforts, although you may be luckier than average and ready to make the best of any situation.

Moon in Virgo

You are endowed with good mental abilities and a keen receptive memory, but you are never ostentatious or pretentious. Naturally quite reserved, you still have many friends, especially of the opposite sex. Marital relationships must be discussed carefully and worked at so that they remain harmonious, as personal attachments can be a problem if you do not give them your full attention.

Talented and persevering, you possess artistic qualities and are a good homemaker. Earning your honours through genuine merit, you work long and hard towards your objectives but show little pride in your achievements. Many short journeys will be undertaken in your life.

Moon in Libra

With the Moon in Libra you are naturally popular and make friends easily. People like you, probably more than you realise, you bring fun to a party and are a natural diplomat. For all its good points, Libra is not the most stable of astrological signs and, as a result, your emotions can be a little unstable too. Therefore, although the Moon in Libra is said to be good for love and marriage, your Sun sign and Rising sign will have an important effect on your emotional and loving qualities.

You must remember to relate to others in your decision-making. Co-operation is crucial because Libra represents the 'balance' of life that can only be achieved through harmonious relationships. Conformity is not easy for you because Libra, an Air sign, likes its independence.

Moon in Scorpio

Some people might call you pushy. In fact, all you really want to do is to live life to the full and protect yourself and your family from the pressures of life. Take care to avoid giving the impression of being sarcastic or impulsive and use your energies wisely and constructively.

You have great courage and you invariably achieve your goals by force of personality and sheer effort. You are fond of mystery and are good at predicting the outcome of situations and events. Travel experiences can be beneficial to you.

You may experience problems if you do not take time to examine your motives in a relationship, and also if you allow jealousy, always a feature of Scorpio, to cloud your judgement.

Moon in Sagittarius

The Moon in Sagittarius helps to make you a generous individual with humanitarian qualities and a kind heart. Restlessness may be intrinsic as your mind is seldom still. Perhaps because of this, you have a need for change that could lead you to several major moves during your adult life. You are not afraid to stand your ground when you know your judgement is right, you speak directly and have good intuition.

At work you are quick, efficient and versatile and so you make an ideal employee. You need work to be intellectually demanding and do not enjoy tedious routines.

In relationships, you anger quickly if faced with stupidity or deception, though you are just as quick to forgive and forget. Emotionally, there are times when your heart rules your head.

Moon in Capricorn

The Moon in Capricorn makes you popular and likely to come into the public eye in some way. The watery Moon is not entirely comfortable in the Earth sign of Capricorn and this may lead to some difficulties in the early years of life. An initial lack of creative ability and indecision must be overcome before the true qualities of patience and perseverance inherent in Capricorn can show through.

You have good administrative ability and are a capable worker, and if you are careful you can accumulate wealth. But you must be cautious and take professional advice in partnerships, as you are open to deception. You may be interested in social or welfare work, which suit your organisational skills and sympathy for others.

Moon in Aquarius

The Moon in Aquarius makes you an active and agreeable person with a friendly, easy-going nature. Sympathetic to the needs of others, you flourish in a laid-back atmosphere. You are broad-minded, fair and open to suggestion, although sometimes you have an unconventional quality which others can find hard to understand.

You are interested in the strange and curious, and in old articles and places. You enjoy trips to these places and gain much from them. Political, scientific and educational work interests you and you might choose a career in science or technology.

Money-wise, you make gains through innovation and concentration and Lunar Aquarians often tackle more than one job at a time. In love you are kind and honest.

Moon in Pisces

You have a kind, sympathetic nature, somewhat retiring at times, but you always take account of others' feelings and help when you can.

Personal relationships may be problematic, but as life goes on you can learn from your experiences and develop a better understanding of yourself and the world around you.

You have a fondness for travel, appreciate beauty and harmony and hate disorder and strife. You may be fond of literature and would make a good writer or speaker yourself. You have a creative imagination and may come across as an incurable romantic. You have strong intuition, maybe bordering on a mediumistic quality, which sets you apart from the mass. You may not be rich in cash terms, but your personal gifts are worth more than gold.

SAGITTARIUS IN LOVE

Discover how compatible in love you are with people from the same and other signs of the zodiac. Five stars equals a match made in heaven!

Sagittarius meets Sagittarius

Although perhaps not the very best partnership for Sagittarius, this must rank as one of the most eventful, electrifying and interesting of the bunch. They will think alike, which is often the key to any relationship but, unfortunately, they may be so busy leading their own lives that they don't spend much time together. Their social life should be something special, and there could be lots of travel. However, domestic responsibilities need to be carefully shared and the family might benefit from a helping hand in this area. Star rating: ****

Sagittarius meets Capricorn

Any real problem here will stem from a lack of understanding. Capricorn is very practical and needs to be constantly on the go, though in a fairly low-key sort of way. Sagittarius is busy too, though always in a panic and invariably behind its deadlines, which will annoy organised Capricorn. Sagittarius doesn't really have the depth of nature that best suits an Earth sign like Capricorn and its flirty nature could upset the sensitive Goat, though its lighter attitude could be cheering, too. Star rating: ***

Sagittarius meets Aquarius

Both Sagittarius and Aquarius are into mind games, which may lead to something of an intellectual competition. If one side is happy to be bamboozled it won't be a problem, but it is more likely that the relationship will turn into a competition which won't auger well for its long-term future. However, on the plus side, both signs are adventurous and sociable, so as long as there is always something new and interesting to do, the match could end up turning out very well. Star rating: **

Sagittarius meets Pisces

Probably the least likely success story for either sign, which is why it scores so low on the star rating. The basic problem is an almost total lack of understanding. A successful relationship needs empathy and progress towards a shared goal but, although both are eager to please, Pisces is too deep and Sagittarius too flighty – they just don't belong on the same planet! As pals, they have more in common and so a friendship is the best hope of success and happiness. Star rating: *

Sagittarius meets Aries

This can be one of the most favourable matches of them all. Both Aries and Sagittarius are Fire signs, which often leads to clashes of will, but this pair find a mutual understanding. Sagittarius helps Aries to develop a better sense of humour, while Aries teaches the Archer about consistency on the road to success. Some patience is called for on both sides, but these people have a natural liking for each other. Add this to growing love and you have a long-lasting combination that is hard to beat. Star rating: *****

Sagittarius meets Taurus

On first impression, Taurus may not like Sagittarius, which may seem brash, and even common, when viewed through the Bull's refined eyes. But, there is hope of success because the two signs have so much to offer each other. The Archer is enthralled by the Taurean's natural poise and beauty, while Taurus always needs more basic confidence, which is no problem to Sagittarius who has plenty to spare. Both signs love to travel. There are certain to be ups and downs, but that doesn't prevent an interesting, inspiring and even exciting combination. Star rating: ***

Sagittarius meets Gemini

A paradoxical relationship this. On paper, the two signs have much in common, but unfortunately, they are often so alike that life turns into a fiercely fought competition. Both signs love change and diversity and both want to be the life and soul of the party. But in life there must always be a leader and a follower, and neither of this pair wants to be second. Both also share a tendency towards infidelity, which may develop into a problem as time passes. This could be an interesting match, but not necessarily successful. Star rating: **

Sagittarius meets Cancer

Although probably not an immediate success, there is hope for this couple. It's hard to see how this pair could get together, because they have few mutual interests. Sagittarius is always on the go, loves a hectic social life and dances the night away. Cancer prefers the cinema or a concert. But, having met, Cancer will appreciate the Archer's happy and cheerful nature, while Sagittarius finds Cancer alluring and intriguing and, as the saying goes, opposites attract. A long-term relationship would focus on commitment to family, with Cancer leading this area. Star rating: ***

Sagittarius meets Leo

An excellent match as Leo and Sagittarius have so much in common. Their general approach to life is very similar, although as they are both Fire signs they can clash impressively! Sagittarius is shallower and more flippant than Leo likes to think of itself, and the Archer will be the one taking emotional chances. Sagittarius has met its match in the Lion's den, as brave Leo won't be outdone by anyone. Financially, they will either be very wealthy or struggling, and family life may be chaotic. Problems, like joys, are handled jointly – and that leads to happiness. Star rating: *****

Sagittarius meets Virgo

There can be some quite strange happenings inside this relationship. Sagittarius and Virgo view life so differently there are always new discoveries. Virgo is much more of a home-bird than Sagittarius, but that won't matter if the Archer introduces its hectic social life gradually. More importantly, Sagittarius understands that it takes Virgo a long time to free its hidden 'inner sprite', but once free it will be fun all the way – until Virgo's thrifty nature takes over. There are great possibilities, but effort is required. Star rating: ***

Sagittarius meets Libra

Libra and Sagittarius are both adaptable signs who get on well with most people, but this promising outlook often does not follow through because each brings out the 'flighty' side of the other. This combination is great for a fling, but when the romance is over someone needs to see to the practical side of life. Both signs are well meaning, pleasant and kind, but are either of them constant enough to build a life together? In at least some cases, the answer would be no. Star rating: ***

Sagittarius meets Scorpio

Sagittarius needs constant stimulation and loves to be busy from dawn till dusk which may mean that it feels rather frustrated by Scorpio. Scorpions are hard workers, too, but they are also contemplative and need periods of quiet which may mean that they appear dull to Sagittarius. This could lead to a gulf between the two which must be overcome. With time and patience on both sides, this can be a lucrative encounter and good in terms of home and family. A variable alliance. Star rating: ***

VENUS:
THE PLANET OF LOVE

If you look up at the sky around sunset or sunrise you will often see Venus in close attendance to the Sun. It is arguably one of the most beautiful sights of all and there is little wonder that historically it became associated with the goddess of love. But although Venus does play an important part in the way you view love and in the way others see you romantically, this is only one of the spheres of influence that it enjoys in your overall character.

Venus has a part to play in the more cultured side of your life and has much to do with your appreciation of art, literature, music and general creativity. Even the way you look is responsive to the part of the zodiac that Venus occupied at the start of your life, though this fact is also down to your Sun sign and Ascending sign. If, at the time you were born, Venus occupied one of the more gregarious zodiac signs, you will be more likely to wear your heart on your sleeve, as well as to be more attracted to entertainment, social gatherings and good company. If on the other hand Venus occupied a quiet zodiac sign at the time of your birth, you would tend to be more retiring and less willing to shine in public situations.

It's good to know what part the planet Venus plays in your life for it can have a great bearing on the way you appear to the rest of the world and since we all have to mix with others, you can learn to make the very best of what Venus has to offer you.

One of the great complications in the past has always been trying to establish exactly what zodiac position Venus enjoyed when you were born because the planet is notoriously difficult to track. However, I have solved that problem by creating a table that is exclusive to your Sun sign, which you will find on the following page.

Establishing your Venus sign could not be easier. Just look up the year of your birth on the page opposite and you will see a sign of the zodiac. This was the sign that Venus occupied in the period covered by your sign in that year. If Venus occupied more than one sign during the period, this is indicated by the date on which the sign changed, and the name of the new sign. For instance, if you were born in 1950, Venus was in Sagittarius until the 16th December, after which time it was in Capricorn. If you were born before 16th December your Venus sign is Sagittarius, if you were born on or after 16th December, your Venus sign is Capricorn. Once you have established the position of Venus at the time of your birth, you can then look in the pages which follow to see how this has a bearing on your life as a whole.

1910 SCORPIO / 24.11 SAGITTARIUS / 18.12 CAPRICORN
1911 LIBRA / 8.12 SCORPIO
1912 CAPRICORN / 13.12 AQUARIUS
1913 SCORPIO / 8.12 SAGITTARIUS
1914 SAGITTARIUS / 6.12 SCORPIO
1915 SAGITTARIUS / 3.12 CAPRICORN
1916 LIBRA / 27.11 SCORPIO
1917 CAPRICORN / 6.12 AQUARIUS
1918 SAGITTARIUS / 18.12 CAPRICORN
1919 LIBRA / 9.12 SCORPIO
1920 CAPRICORN / 13.12 AQUARIUS
1921 SCORPIO / 7.12 SAGITTARIUS
1922 SAGITTARIUS / 29.11 SCORPIO
1923 SAGITTARIUS / 2.12 CAPRICORN
1924 LIBRA / 27.11 SCORPIO
1925 CAPRICORN / 6.12 AQUARIUS
1926 SAGITTARIUS / 17.12 CAPRICORN
1927 LIBRA / 9.12 SCORPIO
1928 CAPRICORN / 13.12 AQUARIUS
1929 SCORPIO / 7.12 SAGITTARIUS
1930 SCORPIO
1931 SAGITTARIUS / 2.12 CAPRICORN
1932 LIBRA / 26.11 SCORPIO
1933 CAPRICORN / 6.12 AQUARIUS
1934 SAGITTARIUS / 17.12 CAPRICORN
1935 LIBRA / 10.12 SCORPIO
1936 CAPRICORN / 12.12 AQUARIUS
1937 SCORPIO / 6.12 SAGITTARIUS
1938 SCORPIO
1939 SAGITTARIUS / 1.12 CAPRICORN
1940 LIBRA / 26.11 SCORPIO
1941 CAPRICORN / 6.12 AQUARIUS
1942 SAGITTARIUS / 16.12 CAPRICORN
1943 LIBRA / 10.12 SCORPIO
1944 CAPRICORN / 12.12 AQUARIUS
1945 SCORPIO / 6.12 SAGITTARIUS
1946 SCORPIO
1947 SAGITTARIUS / 1.12 CAPRICORN
1948 LIBRA / 25.11 SCORPIO / 20.12 SAGITTARIUS
1949 CAPRICORN / 7.12 AQUARIUS
1950 SAGITTARIUS / 16.12 CAPRICORN
1951 LIBRA / 10.12 SCORPIO
1952 CAPRICORN / 11.12 AQUARIUS
1953 SCORPIO / 5.12 SAGITTARIUS
1954 SCORPIO
1955 SAGITTARIUS / 30.11 CAPRICORN
1956 LIBRA / 25.11 SCORPIO / 20.12 SAGITTARIUS
1957 CAPRICORN / 8.12 AQUARIUS
1958 SAGITTARIUS / 15.12 CAPRICORN
1959 LIBRA / 10.12 SCORPIO

1960 CAPRICORN / 11.12 AQUARIUS
1961 SCORPIO / 5.12 SAGITTARIUS
1962 SCORPIO
1963 SAGITTARIUS / 30.11 CAPRICORN
1964 LIBRA / 24.11 SCORPIO / 19.12 SAGITTARIUS
1965 CAPRICORN / 8.12 AQUARIUS
1966 SAGITTARIUS / 15.12 CAPRICORN
1967 LIBRA / 10.12 SCORPIO
1968 CAPRICORN / 10.12 AQUARIUS
1969 SCORPIO / 4.12 SAGITTARIUS
1970 SCORPIO
1971 SAGITTARIUS / 29.11 CAPRICORN
1972 LIBRA / 24.11 SCORPIO / 19.12 SAGITTARIUS
1973 CAPRICORN / 9.12 AQUARIUS
1974 SAGITTARIUS / 14.12 CAPRICORN
1975 LIBRA / 9.12 SCORPIO
1976 CAPRICORN / 9.12 AQUARIUS
1977 SCORPIO / 4.12 SAGITTARIUS
1978 SCORPIO
1979 SAGITTARIUS / 28.11 CAPRICORN
1980 SCORPIO / 18.12 SAGITTARIUS
1981 CAPRICORN / 10.12 AQUARIUS
1982 SAGITTARIUS / 14.12 CAPRICORN
1983 LIBRA / 9.12 SCORPIO
1984 CAPRICORN / 9.12 AQUARIUS
1985 SCORPIO / 3.12 SAGITTARIUS
1986 SCORPIO
1987 SAGITTARIUS / 28.11 CAPRICORN
1988 SCORPIO / 18.12 SAGITTARIUS
1989 CAPRICORN / 11.12 AQUARIUS
1990 SAGITTARIUS / 13.12 CAPRICORN
1991 LIBRA / 9.12 SCORPIO
1992 CAPRICORN / 9.12 AQUARIUS
1993 SCORPIO / 3.12 SAGITTARIUS
1994 SCORPIO
1995 SAGITTARIUS / 28.11 CAPRICORN
1996 SCORPIO / 17.12 SAGITTARIUS
1997 CAPRICORN / 12.12 AQUARIUS
1998 SAGITTARIUS / 13.12 CAPRICORN
1999 LIBRA / 9.12 SCORPIO
2000 CAPRICORN / 8.12 AQUARIUS
2001 SCORPIO / 3.12 SAGITTARIUS
2002 SCORPIO
2003 SAGITTARIUS/28.11 CAPRICORN
2004 SCORPIO / 17.12 SAGITTARIUS
2005 CAPRICORN / 12.12 AQUARIUS
2006 SAGITTARIUS / 13.12 CAPRICORN
2007 LIBRA / 9.12 SCORPIO
2008 CAPRICORN / 8.12 AQUARIUS

VENUS THROUGH THE ZODIAC SIGNS

Venus in Aries

Amongst other things, the position of Venus in Aries indicates a fondness for travel, music and all creative pursuits. Your nature tends to be affectionate and you would try not to create confusion or difficulty for others if it could be avoided. Many people with this planetary position have a great love of the theatre, and mental stimulation is of the greatest importance. Early romantic attachments are common with Venus in Aries, so it is very important to establish a genuine sense of romantic continuity. Early marriage is not recommended, especially if it is based on sympathy. You may give your heart a little too readily on occasions.

Venus in Taurus

You are capable of very deep feelings and your emotions tend to last for a very long time. This makes you a trusting partner and lover, whose constancy is second to none. In life you are precise and careful and always try to do things the right way. Although this means an ordered life, which you are comfortable with, it can also lead you to be rather too fussy for your own good. Despite your pleasant nature, you are very fixed in your opinions and quite able to speak your mind. Others are attracted to you and historical astrologers always quoted this position of Venus as being very fortunate in terms of marriage. However, if you find yourself involved in a failed relationship, it could take you a long time to trust again.

Venus in Gemini

As with all associations related to Gemini, you tend to be quite versatile, anxious for change and intelligent in your dealings with the world at large. You may gain money from more than one source but you are equally good at spending it. There is an inference here that you are a good communicator, via either the written or the spoken word, and you love to be in the company of interesting people. Always on the look-out for culture, you may also be very fond of music, and love to indulge the curious and cultured side of your nature. In romance you tend to have more than one relationship and could find yourself associated with someone who has previously been a friend or even a distant relative.

Venus in Cancer

You often stay close to home because you are very fond of family and enjoy many of your most treasured moments when you are with those you love. Being naturally sympathetic, you will always do anything you can to support those around you, even people you hardly know at all. This charitable side of your nature is your most noticeable trait and is one of the reasons why others are naturally so fond of you. Being receptive and in some cases even psychic, you can see through to the soul of most of those with whom you come into contact. You may not commence too many romantic attachments but when you do give your heart, it tends to be unconditionally.

Venus in Leo

It must become quickly obvious to almost anyone you meet that you are kind, sympathetic and yet determined enough to stand up for anyone or anything that is truly important to you. Bright and sunny, you warm the world with your natural enthusiasm and would rarely do anything to hurt those around you, or at least not intentionally. In romance you are ardent and sincere, though some may find your style just a little overpowering. Gains come through your contacts with other people and this could be especially true with regard to romance, for love and money often come hand in hand for those who were born with Venus in Leo. People claim to understand you, though you are more complex than you seem.

Venus in Virgo

Your nature could well be fairly quiet no matter what your Sun sign might be, though this fact often manifests itself as an inner peace and would not prevent you from being basically sociable. Some delays and even the odd disappointment in love cannot be ruled out with this planetary position, though it's a fact that you will usually find the happiness you look for in the end. Catapulting yourself into romantic entanglements that you know to be rather ill-advised is not sensible, and it would be better to wait before you committed yourself exclusively to any one person. It is the essence of your nature to serve the world at large and through doing so it is possible that you will attract money at some stage in your life.

Venus in Libra

Venus is very comfortable in Libra and bestows upon those people who have this planetary position a particular sort of kindness that is easy to recognise. This is a very good position for all sorts of friendships and also for romantic attachments that usually bring much joy into your life. Few individuals with Venus in Libra would avoid marriage and since you are capable of great depths of love, it is likely that you will find a contented personal life. You like to mix with people of integrity and intelligence but don't take kindly to scruffy surroundings or work that means getting your hands too dirty. Careful speculation, good business dealings and money through marriage all seem fairly likely.

Venus in Scorpio

You are quite open and tend to spend money quite freely, even on those occasions when you don't have very much. Although your intentions are always good, there are times when you get yourself in to the odd scrape and this can be particularly true when it comes to romance, which you may come to late or from a rather unexpected direction. Certainly you have the power to be happy and to make others contented on the way, but you find the odd stumbling block on your journey through life and it could seem that you have to work harder than those around you. As a result of this, you gain a much deeper understanding of the true value of personal happiness than many people ever do, and are likely to achieve true contentment in the end.

Venus in Sagittarius

You are lighthearted, cheerful and always able to see the funny side of any situation. These facts enhance your popularity, which is especially high with members of the opposite sex. You should never have to look too far to find romantic interest in your life, though it is just possible that you might be too willing to commit yourself before you are certain that the person in question is right for you. Part of the problem here extends to other areas of life too. The fact is that you like variety in everything and so can tire of situations that fail to offer it. All the same, if you choose wisely and learn to understand your restless side, then great happiness can be yours.

Venus in Capricorn

The most notable trait that comes from Venus in this position is that it makes you trustworthy and able to take on all sorts of responsibilities in life. People are instinctively fond of you and love you all the more because you are always ready to help those who are in any form of need. Social and business popularity can be yours and there is a magnetic quality to your nature that is particularly attractive in a romantic sense. Anyone who wants a partner for a lover, a spouse and a good friend too would almost certainly look in your direction. Constancy is the hallmark of your nature and unfaithfulness would go right against the grain. You might sometimes be a little too trusting.

Venus in Aquarius

This location of Venus offers a fondness for travel and a desire to try out something new at every possible opportunity. You are extremely easy to get along with and tend to have many friends from varied backgrounds, classes and inclinations. You like to live a distinct sort of life and gain a great deal from moving about, both in a career sense and with regard to your home. It is not out of the question that you could form a romantic attachment to someone who comes from far away or be attracted to a person of a distinctly artistic and original nature. What you cannot stand is jealousy, for you have friends of both sexes and would want to keep things that way.

Venus in Pisces

The first thing people tend to notice about you is your wonderful, warm smile. Being very charitable by nature you will do anything to help others, even if you don't know them well. Much of your life may be spent sorting out situations for other people, but it is very important to feel that you are living for yourself too. In the main, you remain cheerful, and tend to be quite attractive to members of the opposite sex. Where romantic attachments are concerned, you could be drawn to people who are significantly older or younger than yourself or to someone with a unique career or point of view. It might be best for you to avoid marrying whilst you are still very young.

THE ASTRAL DIARY
HOW THE DIAGRAMS WORK

Through the picture diagrams in the Astral Diary I want to help you to plot your year. With them you can see where the positive and negative aspects will be found in each month. To make the most of them, all you have to do is remember where and when!

Let me show you how they work ...

THE MONTH AT A GLANCE

Just as there are twelve separate zodiac signs, so astrologers believe that each sign has twelve separate aspects to life. Each of the twelve segments relates to a different personal aspect. I list them all every month so that their meanings are always clear.

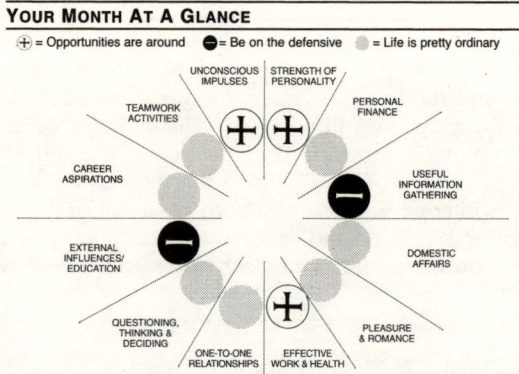

I have designed this chart to show you how and when these twelve different aspects are being influenced throughout the year. When there is a shaded circle, nothing out of the ordinary is to be expected. However, when a circle turns white with a plus sign, the influence is positive. Where the circle is black with a minus sign, it is a negative.

YOUR ENERGY RHYTHM CHART

On the opposite page is a picture diagram in which I am linking your zodiac group to the rhythm of the Moon. In doing this I have calculated when you will be gaining strength from its influence and equally when you may be weakened by it.

If you think of yourself as being like the tides of the ocean then you may understand how your own energies must also rise and fall. And if you understand how it works and when it is working, then you can better organise your activities to achieve more and get things done more easily.

YOUR ENERGY RHYTHM CHART

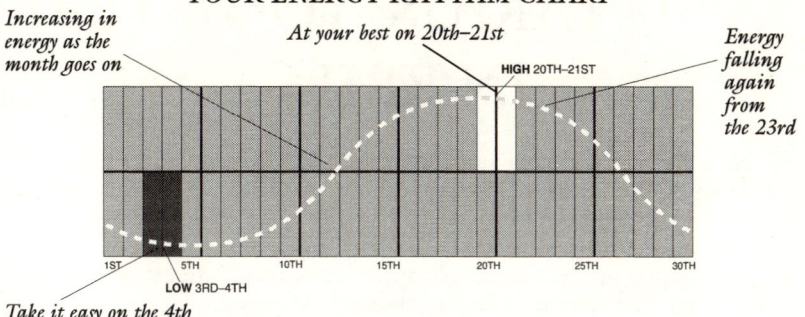

Increasing in energy as the month goes on

At your best on 20th–21st

HIGH 20TH–21ST

Energy falling again from the 23rd

LOW 3RD–4TH

Take it easy on the 4th

MOVING PICTURE SCREEN
Love, money, career and vitality measured every week

The diagram at the end of each week is designed to be informative and fun. The arrows move up and down the scale to give you an idea of the strength of your opportunities in each area. If LOVE stands at plus 4, then get out and put yourself about because things are going your way in romance! The further down the arrow goes, the weaker the opportunities. Do note that the diagram is an overall view of your astrological aspects and therefore reflects a trend which may not concur with every day in that cycle.

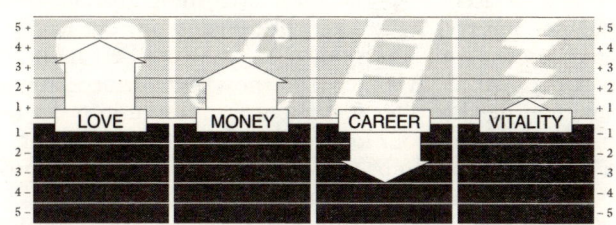

AND FINALLY:

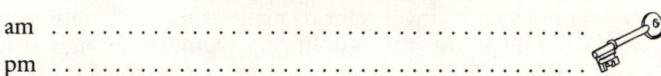

am ....

pm ....

The two lines that are left blank in each daily entry of the Astral Diary are for your own personal use. You may find them ideal for keeping a check on birthdays or appointments, though it could be an idea to make notes from the astrological trends and diagrams a few weeks in advance. Some of the lines are marked with a key, which indicates the working of astrological cycles in your life. Look out for them each week as they are the best days to take action or make decisions. The daily text tells you which area of your life to focus on.

☿ = Mercury is retrograde on that day.

SAGITTARIUS: YOUR YEAR IN BRIEF

There are no real shortcuts at the start of this year, and if you want things to work out well for you during January and February you will have to put in that extra bit of effort that can make all the difference later. Stay in touch with people from the past, especially colleagues, because they might play an important role again soon. Love interest is stimulated in February with new relationships possible for some.

With March and April comes an ever-greater desire to stretch credibility and to get on well, especially at work. Things should be fairly plain sailing on the home front, but not everyone will behave in quite the way you might expect. Money matters are likely to be stronger and there could be more cash about than you will have expected. Use it as wisely as you can and don't be inclined to splash out on luxuries you don't need and probably don't even want all that much.

The arrival of the summer finds you on top form. Throughout May and June you are likely to be socialising a great deal and will be up for almost anything that your friends can suggest. Sagittarius is even more courageous than usual at this time, but a little care is necessary in June because you might be slightly accident-prone. Not everything that happens will be strictly planned, but you are excellent at thinking on your feet.

July and August could turn out to be the very best months as far as change is concerned. With some restlessness quite evident in your nature at this time you need to alter just about everything in order to be even reasonably content with your lot. Waves of new experiences are breaking over you but these prove to be very significant and you react positively to new responsibilities and even new attachments.

The autumn could prove to be the best time for travel for at least some Archers, and a holiday taken during September could turn out to be not just enjoyable but deeply memorable too. You will still not be happy to let sleeping dogs lie and will want to make as many alterations to your life as you can. This is also the case during October, though at least by this time you will be slightly more settled from a personal point of view.

The end of the year could prove to be somewhat quieter and will offer slightly more time for reflection, though even this is relative bearing in mind the Sagittarian nature. November and December bring personal enjoyment, some financial gain and a great deal of promise for future efforts. When you need help you can find it, and you have what it takes to build a really super Christmas for your family and friends. As always you live your life at a fantastic speed, but the festive season ought to offer at least a little time to recharge your batteries.

January 2008

YOUR MONTH AT A GLANCE

⊕ = Opportunities are around   ⊖ = Be on the defensive   ● = Life is pretty ordinary

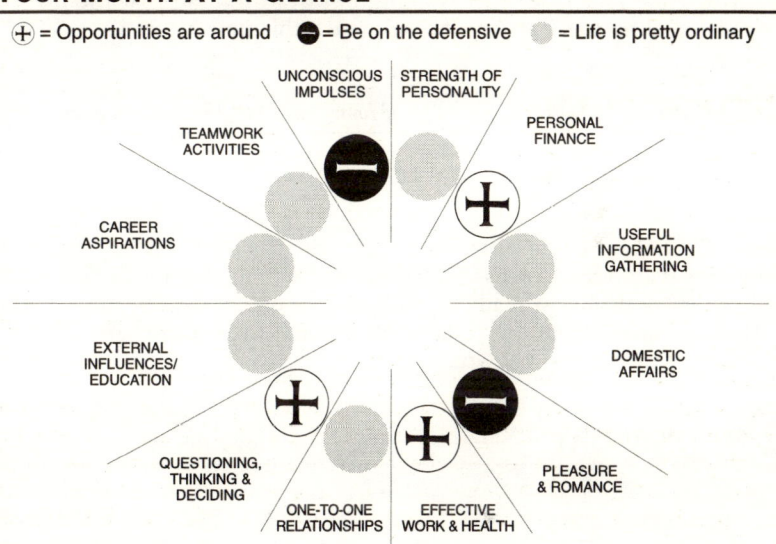

JANUARY HIGHS AND LOWS

Here I show you how the rhythms of the Moon will affect you this month.
Like the tide, your energies and abilities will rise and fall with its pattern.
When it is above the centre line, go for it, when it is below, you should be
resting.

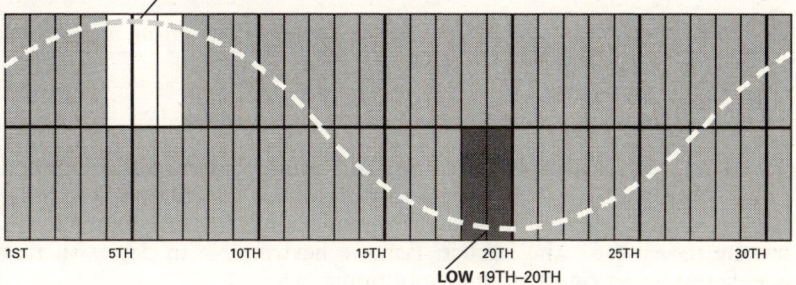

HIGH 5TH–7TH

LOW 19TH–20TH

41

31 MONDAY
Moon Age Day 22   Moon Sign Libra

am . . . .

pm . . . .
The last day of the year offers you an opportunity to dream up ever more exciting possibilities for the new year. You can contribute well to any festivities that take place this evening, but bear in mind that the planets favour a slightly more abstemious approach this time around!

1 TUESDAY
Moon Age Day 23   Moon Sign Libra

am . . . .

pm . . . .
You can make things fairly interesting on the first day of the year, especially if ambitious plans you have been holding over for the last week or two are now almost ready to be launched on an unsuspecting world. If there are any frustrations today these come along because you can't get cracking as quickly as you would wish.

2 WEDNESDAY
Moon Age Day 24   Moon Sign Libra

am . . . .

pm . . . .
If your ego needs something of a boost at the moment, it's worth seeking it from either family members, friends or most likely, colleagues. Now fully back into the swing of things you have scope to show everyone just what you can do. Small financial gains are possible today, but speculation should be limited.

3 THURSDAY
Moon Age Day 25   Moon Sign Scorpio

am . . . .

pm . . . .
Travel matters need extra attention and some Sagittarians could find things quieter today. This is because the Moon has entered your solar twelfth house, supporting a slightly more contemplative time than is usually the case for the Archer. For the next couple of days you may decide not to act on impulse or intuition.

4 FRIDAY
Moon Age Day 26   Moon Sign Scorpio

am . . . .

pm . . . .
A day to keep watching and waiting, because even if you are not exactly pushing for all you are worth, there should still be moments when the time is right to act. The focus is now on family members, and you have what it takes to guide a younger person along a more sensible path then the one they are choosing.

5 SATURDAY
Moon Age Day 27   Moon Sign Sagittarius

am . . . .

pm . . . .
The Moon returns to your own zodiac sign of Sagittarius, bringing that part of the month known as the lunar high. This is the time to act and a three-day period during which you can really get things going your way. Sagittarius doesn't usually take much in the way of encouragement, so use this positive weekend to your advantage.

6 SUNDAY
Moon Age Day 28   Moon Sign Sagittarius

am . . . .

pm . . . .
This is another day for letting go and allowing yourself to shine. People love to have you around and especially so right now. If there are no specific invitations that sound like fun, invent something yourself. You can persuade friends to join in and can even make a very positive impression on strangers under present trends.

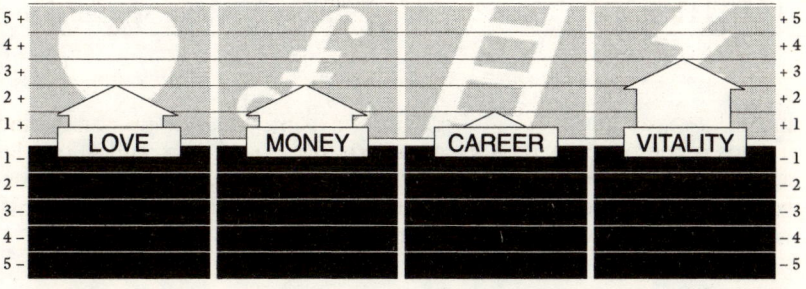

7 MONDAY   *Moon Age Day 29   Moon Sign Sagittarius*

am . . . .

pm . . . .
During the first half of today at least the Moon remains in your own
zodiac sign, so the start of the working week should be extremely positive
and offers new incentives. Things could quieten somewhat later, but by
that time you should have gained extra momentum. An ideal time to
contact friends at a distance.

8 TUESDAY   *Moon Age Day 0   Moon Sign Capricorn*

am . . . .

pm . . . .
There is just a slight danger at the moment that you could be arguing for
your limitations, and that is not a good way for Sagittarius to be. Even
on those occasions when you are not absolutely sure of yourself it is
important to act as though you are. Romance could be high on your
agenda, and new possibilities beckon for some.

9 WEDNESDAY   *Moon Age Day 1   Moon Sign Capricorn*

am . . . .

pm . . . .
Good times are achievable at home, though you may now be slightly less
socially inclined and might easily settle for the fireside. This is fairly
unusual for the Archer, but a short rest does you no harm at all. It won't
be long before you can get back in the thick of things again and push on
towards the next bright idea.

10 THURSDAY   *Moon Age Day 2   Moon Sign Aquarius*

am . . . .

pm . . . .
Trends encourage you to seek reassurance from loved ones, and since you
are not always as certain of yourself as you pretend to be, this should be
very welcome. The only slight fly in the ointment today could come if
you have to defer your own ideas in favour of those of a colleague.

11 FRIDAY
Moon Age Day 3   Moon Sign Aquarius

am . . . .

pm . . . .
A day to welcome people you don't see all that often into your life. There could also be a number of peculiar coincidences taking place and a generally weird feel to certain aspects of life. All of this is going to be fascinating to the average Sagittarian and should keep you fully occupied.

12 SATURDAY
Moon Age Day 4   Moon Sign Pisces

am . . . .

pm . . . .
The present position of Mars in your solar chart assists you to be slightly more critical and inclined to speak your mind, even when you are not asked to do so. It doesn't take much to get the Archer talking, but not everything you say will be all that welcome. It might be good to count to ten on occasions.

13 SUNDAY
Moon Age Day 5   Moon Sign Pisces

am . . . .

pm . . . .
Relationships can benefit from a very positive lift today – though only certain attachments. You might be far more attracted to old and trusted friends than you will be to either colleagues or acquaintances. It might be best not to work on this particular Sunday if you have any choice in the matter. Leisure works best now.

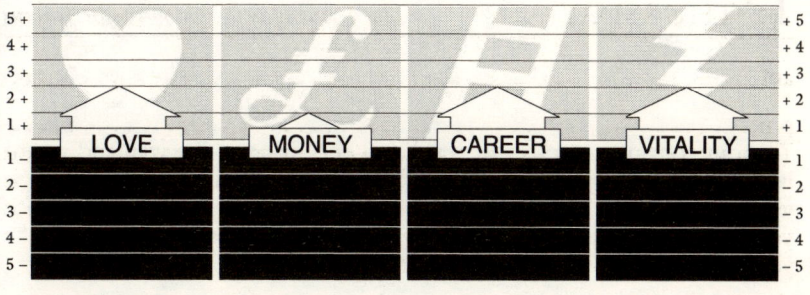

14 MONDAY
Moon Age Day 6   Moon Sign Pisces

am . . . .

pm . . . .
The greater the exchange of ideas today, the better you can make the day go for you. Any slight hiccups from yesterday can soon be forgotten because nothing lasts very long in the Sagittarian life. Now you simply want to co-operate and to show the world how capable you can be. Your nature can be charming and you should have time for everyone.

15 TUESDAY
Moon Age Day 7   Moon Sign Aries

am . . . .

pm . . . .
There are many possible directions to take just at the moment and since you are spoiled for choice it might be good to seek some outside advice. Your best approach is to turn towards old friends and wise family members. Trust is a particularly important factor at the moment and is something you should understand well.

16 WEDNESDAY
Moon Age Day 8   Moon Sign Aries

am . . . .

pm . . . .
You have what it takes to start something completely new – even if certain other people think you are quite mad. The Archer cannot abide standing still for any length of time and there won't be a moment to lose when it comes to furthering your own interests. Finances may be variable, but better if you avoid dodgy speculations.

17 THURSDAY
Moon Age Day 9   Moon Sign Taurus

am . . . .

pm . . . .
You can continue to push forward in a very progressive way and might be quite surprised if there are people around who don't automatically go along with your plans. A little persuasion can work wonders, and since you have what it takes to sell refrigerators to Eskimos it shouldn't take you long to get just about everyone onside.

18 FRIDAY

Moon Age Day 10   Moon Sign Taurus

am . . . .

pm . . . .
Does it feel as though you are running out of steam slightly? If you have been keeping up a rather hectic pace since the start of the year, now there are some slightly less favourable planetary trends to deal with. Today is a time to jog along rather than a period for showing your most dynamic side.

19 SATURDAY

Moon Age Day 11   Moon Sign Gemini

am . . . .

pm . . . .
The Moon now enters the zodiac sign of Gemini, which is your opposite sign. This brings the time of the month known as the lunar low. You may not be anywhere near as progressive or certain of yourself as you have been recently, and would be wise to recharge your flagging batteries for a day or two. That can be difficult for the Archer to do.

20 SUNDAY

Moon Age Day 12   Moon Sign Gemini

am . . . .

pm . . . .
Any frustrations that are present today exist not because of the lunar low but rather on account of your response to it. As long as you realise that you sometimes have to watch and wait, there should be little or no problem. Difficulties could arise if you push forward in any case, which is like knocking your head against a brick wall.

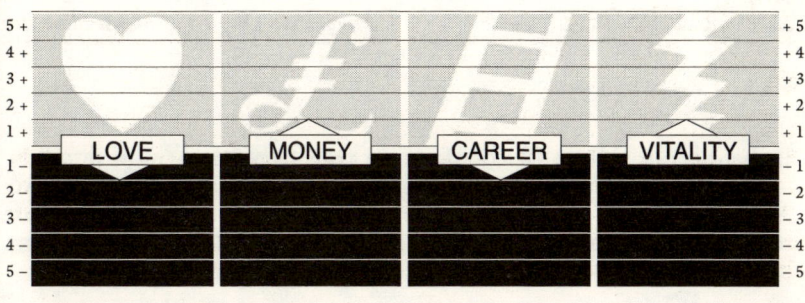

21 MONDAY
Moon Age Day 13   Moon Sign Cancer

am . . . .

pm . . . .
The time is right to get things on the move again and to be more assertive. You could get a great deal from travel and from being in the right place at the best possible time to start something new at work. Self-employed Archers could be in the best position of all right now to move into an entirely different league.

22 TUESDAY
Moon Age Day 14   Moon Sign Cancer

am . . . .

pm . . . .
The green light is on, which offers you plenty of opportunities. No matter what the winter weather is doing you can get out and about, seeing and doing as much as proves to be possible. If you use your energy you shouldn't have any difficulty proving to people that you are the right person for just about any job!

23 WEDNESDAY
Moon Age Day 15   Moon Sign Leo

am . . . .

pm . . . .
Sagittarius gets away with things that just about no other zodiac sign can, and it's all because of your innate cheek and natural charm. You can show your competitive side at present but such is your character that you can find ways of winning, without upsetting anyone on the way. It's just the way you are.

24 THURSDAY
Moon Age Day 16   Moon Sign Leo

am . . . .

pm . . . .
If there is one thing that could get on your nerves right now it will be following rules you see as being both pointless and counter-productive. As a result you could easily fall foul of people who are far more regimented and steady than you are. There isn't much point in arguing because you will have to toe the line in the end.

48

25 FRIDAY
Moon Age Day 17   Moon Sign Virgo

am . . . .

pm . . . .
Once again you can become frustrated if you don't get ahead in the way you would wish, and especially if you sense this is happening because people are deliberately getting in your way. But, as the saying goes, there are more ways than one to skin a cat, and if you use a little psychology you have scope to win out in the end.

26 SATURDAY
Moon Age Day 18   Moon Sign Virgo

am . . . . , ...

pm . . . .
Trends enhance your thought processes, and the weekend should offer you chances to put all this mental energy to good use. What you need most is some fun, and with friends around that shouldn't be too difficult to achieve. Even the presence of the winter weather needn't dampen your spirits at the moment.

27 SUNDAY
Moon Age Day 19   Moon Sign Libra

am . . . .

pm . . . .
A slightly quieter Archer could well greet this particular day, though 'slightly' is probably the operative word. You can use today to get on side with family members, and to prove to your partner just how important they are to you. You can afford to be selfless today.

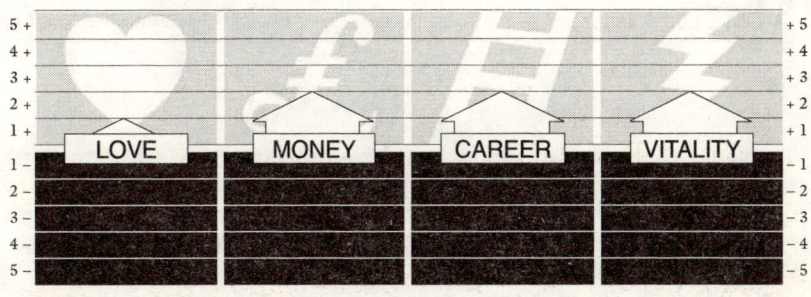

28 MONDAY *Moon Age Day 20 Moon Sign Libra*

am . . . .

pm . . . .
You may not mind at all dealing with the dross today, and have what it takes to be both rational and steadfast. This is so unusual for Sagittarius that it could surprise colleagues and might even astonish you. In a social sense you remain as humorous as ever and have what it takes to be the centre of attention in all public settings.

29 TUESDAY ☿ *Moon Age Day 21 Moon Sign Libra*

am . . . .

pm . . . .
Beware of impulse purchases at the moment, and if possible keep your purse strings firmly tied. This is not necessarily because you are spending more than you can afford, but rather because the real bargains come along in a few days. Any major purchase made today might lead to regret before the weekend arrives.

30 WEDNESDAY ☿ *Moon Age Day 22 Moon Sign Scorpio*

am . . . .

pm . . . .
A day to seek out the support of loved ones and make it easy for them to understand that you are there for them too. If you have been busy out there in the wider world during January, you may have failed to give as much support to family members as you could have done. It's easy to redress the balance now and to show your warmth.

31 THURSDAY ☿ *Moon Age Day 23 Moon Sign Scorpio*

am . . . .

pm . . . .
The last day of January supports a thoughtful interlude when you can mull things over more than would generally be the case. The Moon is in your solar twelfth house, encouraging you to wait a while before embarking on anything new. Today is also ideal for new interests that can only be undertaken alone.

1 FRIDAY
☿ *Moon Age Day 24*   *Moon Sign Sagittarius*

am . . . .

pm . . . .

The lunar high this time around brings a potentially excellent romantic phase into your life. When it comes to impressing someone important you definitely have what it takes to succeed and your attractive nature may even extend in directions you didn't intend. Be prepared to make yourself flavour of the month.

2 SATURDAY
☿ *Moon Age Day 25*   *Moon Sign Sagittarius*

am . . . .

pm . . . .

You can continue to make progress, particularly if you keep Lady Luck on your side at present. Confidence to do the right thing is not lacking and the only slight pity is that the weekend may not offer you the chance to move a few mountains at work. Still, there are other equally fascinating possibilities.

3 SUNDAY
☿ *Moon Age Day 26*   *Moon Sign Sagittarius*

am . . . .

pm . . . .

Continue to follow your own intuition and to encourage other people along the path of life with you. There are all sorts of different individuals around at present and it is the variety in life that captivates you the most. You may well decide to be on the move today and can be at your most impressive when you are in the lead.

	LOVE	MONEY	CAREER	VITALITY
5 +				+ 5
4 +				+ 4
3 +				+ 3
2 +				+ 2
1 +				+ 1
1 −				− 1
2 −				− 2
3 −				− 3
4 −				− 4
5 −				− 5

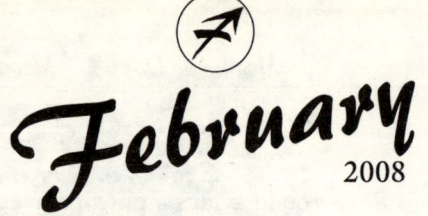

February 2008

YOUR MONTH AT A GLANCE

⊕ = Opportunities are around   ⊖ = Be on the defensive   ⬤ = Life is pretty ordinary

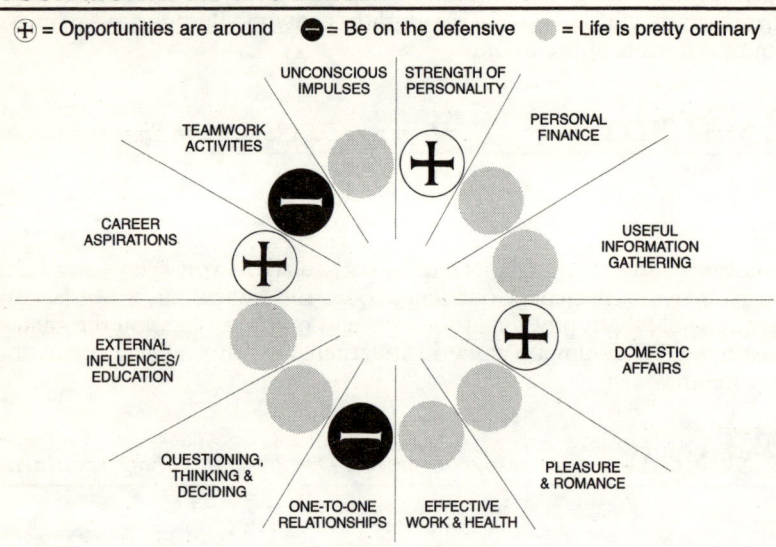

FEBRUARY HIGHS AND LOWS

Here I show you how the rhythms of the Moon will affect you this month. Like the tide, your energies and abilities will rise and fall with its pattern. When it is above the centre line, go for it, when it is below, you should be resting.

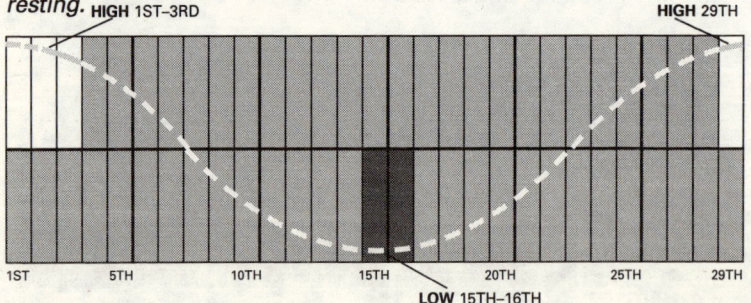

4 MONDAY ☿ *Moon Age Day 27   Moon Sign Capricorn*

am . . . .

pm . . . .
Even if not everyone is on your side at the beginning of this week, that needn't worry you too much. What matters is the individuals who are following your lead, because you will go further at the moment with some support. There are new possibilities to pursue in your working life.

5 TUESDAY ☿ *Moon Age Day 28   Moon Sign Capricorn*

am . . . .

pm . . . .
Someone you know well but see rarely could well be making a return appearance to your life – perhaps to your overwhelming joy. However it's important to remember at the moment that you cannot recreate the past, and if you try too hard to do so there could be problems in the here and now. Better to let sleeping dogs lie if possible.

6 WEDNESDAY ☿ *Moon Age Day 0   Moon Sign Aquarius*

am . . . .

pm . . . .
Keep an open mind about all new possibilities, especially in a professional sense. Fortunately Sagittarius works best on a mixture of common sense and intuition, a combination that can be of great use to you at the moment. Don't get too bogged down with pointless rules and regulations, and remain as original as possible.

7 THURSDAY ☿ *Moon Age Day 1   Moon Sign Aquarius*

am . . . .

pm . . . .
From a social point of view you have what it takes to make the very best of impressions around this part of the week. There could well be an opportunity to mix business with pleasure and to get yourself noticed even more than normal. Someone who has real authority could be calling on your assistance.

8 FRIDAY ☿ *Moon Age Day 2* *Moon Sign Aquarius*

am . . . .

pm . . . .
The romantic possibilities for the Archer look especially good at the moment and you should find it easy to make the best possible impression on others. If you have been on the verge of starting a new relationship but didn't have the courage to ask the right question, now is the time to speak your mind – though in the most romantic way.

9 SATURDAY ☿ *Moon Age Day 3* *Moon Sign Pisces*

am . . . .

pm . . . .
Trends assist you to be in the pink and to be genuinely and consistently funny at present. If you are called upon to speak in public, you can make the best impression possible, though even in a more casual sense, alongside your friends, you can set yourself apart as the most entertaining person present.

10 SUNDAY ☿ *Moon Age Day 4* *Moon Sign Pisces*

am . . . .

pm . . . .
Life responds best to simplicity at present, rather than to intrigues and mysteries. On the whole you would be better off keeping things as routine as possible, whilst at the same time leaving hours free to please yourself and your loved ones.

	LOVE	MONEY	CAREER	VITALITY
5 +				+5
4 +				+4
3 +				+3
2 +				+2
1 +				+1
1 –				–1
2 –				–2
3 –				–3
4 –				–4
5 –				–5

11 MONDAY ☿ *Moon Age Day 5   Moon Sign Aries*

am . . . .

pm . . . .
Anything odd, unusual or curious has potential to attract your attention throughout the first part of this week, and you should be especially well tuned to any coincidences that are firing off around you. These come as signposts to tell you that you are doing the right things and travelling in the most opportune direction.

12 TUESDAY ☿ *Moon Age Day 6   Moon Sign Aries*

am . . . .

pm . . . .
There are signs that mechanical objects might let you down for a day or two and you may decide to call on the help of specialists in order to keep things moving. Don't put yourself in any potential danger by messing with equipment you don't understand and observe sensible precautions, especially when dealing with complicated machinery.

13 WEDNESDAY ☿ *Moon Age Day 7   Moon Sign Taurus*

am . . . .

pm . . . .
All that glistens certainly isn't gold, as you could find out today if you don't pay attention. The best way towards greater financial strength is a steady and continual effort, and you won't get where you want to be with short cuts. There are times when the Archer can make a mint through risks, but not at the moment.

14 THURSDAY ☿ *Moon Age Day 8   Moon Sign Taurus*

am . . . .

pm . . . .
Your responses are far from being standard right now and one of the best ways of getting the attention of important people is to shock them a little. You are sufficiently well balanced at the moment not to go over the top, but if you do nothing you won't stand out from the crowd. It's important for you to get your unique skills noticed.

15 FRIDAY ☿ *Moon Age Day 9   Moon Sign Gemini*

am . . . .

pm . . . .
Trying too hard is not the best use of time whilst the lunar low is around, and you might be much better off simply standing back and allowing others to take the strain. Meanwhile you can take a well-earned rest, whilst planning your strategies for next week. New hobbies or alternative ways of passing your time are on offer around now.

16 SATURDAY ☿ *Moon Age Day 10   Moon Sign Gemini*

am . . . .

pm . . . .
The first part of the weekend at least is hardly likely to inspire you greatly. This is partly because of the lunar low, but can also be affected by the behaviour of others. Rather than getting involved in rows or even deep discussions, consider whether you would be far better off on your own for the moment.

17 SUNDAY ☿ *Moon Age Day 11   Moon Sign Cancer*

am . . . .

pm . . . .
A day to make improvements, and to allow yourself to feel very optimistic. The time still isn't right to act decisively but you can find ways to enjoy yourself, whilst at the same time appealing to the better judgements of those around you. It's time to drum up support for something you are mulling over.

	LOVE	MONEY	CAREER	VITALITY
5 +					+ 5
4 +					+ 4
3 +					+ 3
2 +					+ 2
1 +					+ 1
1 −					− 1
2 −					− 2
3 −					− 3
4 −					− 4
5 −					− 5

18 MONDAY ☿ *Moon Age Day 12   Moon Sign Cancer*

am . . . .

pm . . . .
The Archer has potential to become more and more calculating – which means an unsuspecting world had better watch out. There are gains to be made in the financial arena and you shouldn't easily have the wool pulled over your eyes. Even if few people really understand what sort of an adversary you would make, they could be about to find out!

19 TUESDAY ☿ *Moon Age Day 13   Moon Sign Leo*

am . . . .

pm . . . .
Your strength lies in remaining positive and looking after your own best interests. At the same time you can begin to show the romantic qualities within your nature more than has been the case for a few days. A day to show others just how magnetic and attractive you can be.

20 WEDNESDAY *Moon Age Day 14   Moon Sign Leo*

am . . . .

pm . . . .
Standard responses may not work too well at this stage of the week and you might have to be very original if you want to be noticed. Getting ahead means standing out in a crowd and you have to find new ways to do so. Once again you show a real penchant for anything odd or unusual, and for certain aspects of history.

21 THURSDAY *Moon Age Day 15   Moon Sign Leo*

am . . . .

pm . . . .
You can afford to go along with anything you see as being sensible and for the first time in a while you can get on particularly well in group situations. The dynamics of such gatherings do offer you scope to become the leader rather than following the lead of wishy-washy types.

22 FRIDAY   *Moon Age Day 16   Moon Sign Virgo*

am . . . .

pm . . . .
You can make contact with some fascinating types today and across the
weekend and your thirst for life is difficult to quench at present. Anyone
who is different than the norm has potential to grab your attention and
their presence in your life inspires you to show just how opposed to
convention you are also inclined to be.

23 SATURDAY   *Moon Age Day 17   Moon Sign Virgo*

am . . . .

pm . . . .
Attitude is crucially important when dealing with family members or even
friends who have problems at the moment. You might respond very
positively today to a shopping spree or anything that captivates your
attention rather than simply taking up your time. What you don't care for
right now is too much routine and expectation.

24 SUNDAY   *Moon Age Day 18   Moon Sign Libra*

am . . . .

pm . . . .
The Archer can attract people now because it appears to them that you
have all the answers. Of course this is not the case but you don't have to
tell them that. You can go further on a hunch and a bluff than any other
zodiac sign, and this should become more than obvious right now. Why
not get out into the fresh air and look for simple fun?

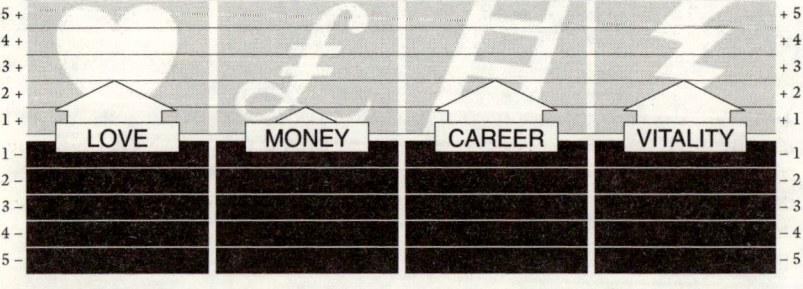

25 MONDAY
Moon Age Day 19   Moon Sign Libra

am . . . .

pm . . . .
With a new week beginning it's worth taking more notice of facts that didn't occur to you a few days ago. You can see clear through the heart of matters and shouldn't be at all fooled by people who are trying to be something they are not. You have what it takes to persuade others to follow your lead, even dynamic types.

26 TUESDAY
Moon Age Day 20   Moon Sign Scorpio

am . . . .

pm . . . .
Stand by to make the most of a couple of much quieter days as the Moon passes through your solar twelfth house. Now you can be more contemplative, less aggressive and more inclined to meditate. This does you no harm at all because amongst your deep thoughts are possibilities that can be turned to your advantage in a few days.

27 WEDNESDAY
Moon Age Day 21   Moon Sign Scorpio

am . . . .

pm . . . .
Even if the middle of the week this time around isn't your most productive or positive phase, it does have the advantage of being steady enough to give you more than enough time to plan ahead. In fact it may look as though some situations are happening in slow motion, though that's just the Sagittarian mind at work.

28 THURSDAY
Moon Age Day 22   Moon Sign Scorpio

am . . . .

pm . . . .
As today advances, so you can move closer to getting your own way big time. You might not actually manage to get what you want absolutely, but you can make sure that things only need the smallest nudge in order to fall your way. The secret lies in not putting on that last, important pressure until the time is exactly right.

29 FRIDAY   *Moon Age Day 23   Moon Sign Sagittarius*

am . . . .

pm . . . .

Now you should act, and do so in the most definite way possible. The lunar high offers scope for better luck, a more dynamic approach and an increase in your general charm. Few people should stand in your way today, either because they genuinely like you enough to do what you want or because they are wary of you and dare not argue!

1 SATURDAY   *Moon Age Day 24   Moon Sign Sagittarius*

am . . . .

pm . . . .

You continue to show what you are made of and won't take no for an answer. This is fine for you but rather difficult for some of the people you are dealing with today. Go for gold but at the same time understand that not everyone can keep up with your level of activity or your lightning-quick thought processes. Romance is favoured.

2 SUNDAY   *Moon Age Day 25   Moon Sign Capricorn*

am . . . .

pm . . . .

You can now slow things down again, which is no bad thing considering how frenetic life has been for the last couple of days. Suddenly events begin to happen that are beyond your own influence and you seem to be caught up in magical happenings that seem as though they come from a storybook. This can be an enchanting time.

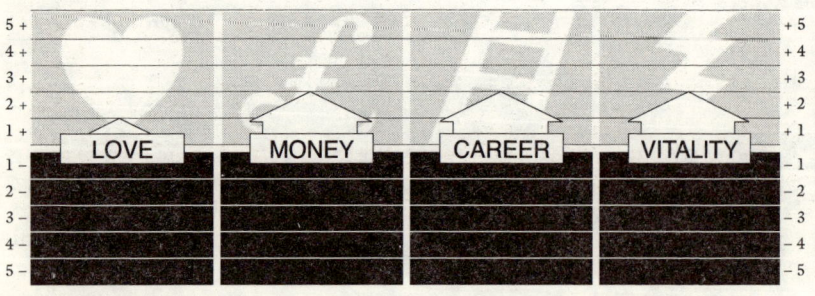

March 2008

YOUR MONTH AT A GLANCE

⊕ = Opportunities are around   ⊖ = Be on the defensive   ⬤ = Life is pretty ordinary

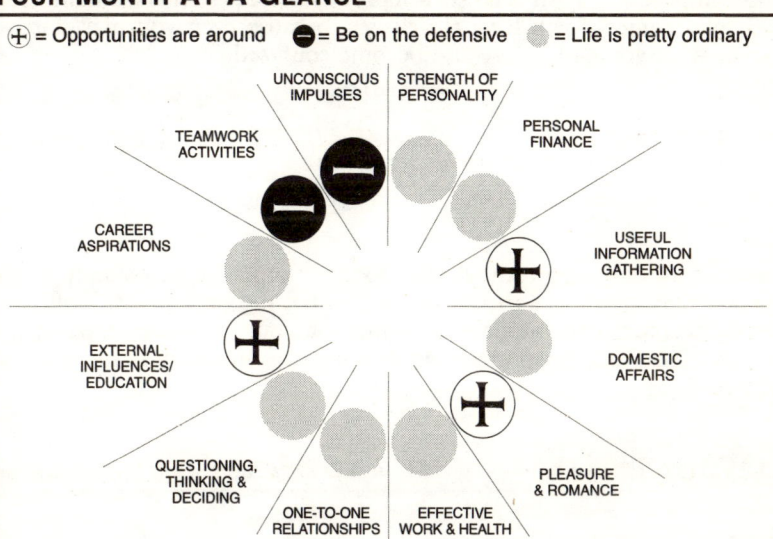

MARCH HIGHS AND LOWS

Here I show you how the rhythms of the Moon will affect you this month. Like the tide, your energies and abilities will rise and fall with its pattern. When it is above the centre line, go for it, when it is below, you should be resting.

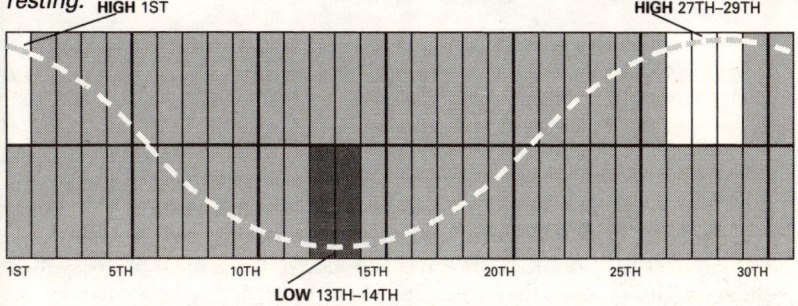

HIGH 1ST   HIGH 27TH–29TH

1ST   5TH   10TH   15TH   20TH   25TH   30TH

LOW 13TH–14TH

3 MONDAY
Moon Age Day 26   Moon Sign Capricorn

am . . . .

pm . . . .
It may be necessary to keep up some sort of pretence if you want to maintain your street-cred right now. To many people this would make life too complicated, but it is no sort of problem to the Archer. The only real difficulty comes if you have to tell lies, because even you may start to forget what you said before and become confused.

4 TUESDAY
Moon Age Day 27   Moon Sign Capricorn

am . . . .

pm . . . .
Instead of going round the houses today it might be best simply to ask for what you want and then wait to see what the response is. Don't get overconcerned with the details of situations but go to the heart of the matter if you can. Sagittarians can now take advantage of better physical trends.

5 WEDNESDAY
Moon Age Day 28   Moon Sign Aquarius

am . . . .

pm . . . .
Mid-week blues could well come along and threaten to spoil something you have been anticipating. The best way round this is to keep active and to pitch in and help someone else. If you remain busy you should no longer have time to think about your own lack of sparkle, to such an extent that you can soon get it back!

6 THURSDAY
Moon Age Day 29   Moon Sign Aquarius

am . . . .

pm . . . .
This is a time during which home and family are to the fore. There may be plans around for holidays that will come later in the year, and for some lucky Archers the potential for travel is good right now. An out-of-season holiday might appeal to you, but any sort of journey is well starred now.

7 FRIDAY
Moon Age Day 0   Moon Sign Pisces

am . . . .

pm . . . .
By all means get cracking with things you understand, but stay away from complications and mysteries because these could complicate your life for the moment. Attitude is very important when dealing with colleagues and especially with superiors. The more you strive to build bridges, the better things are likely to turn out for you.

8 SATURDAY
Moon Age Day 1   Moon Sign Pisces

am . . . .

pm . . . .
This is a Saturday that works best for Archers who are willing to take a chance. Sitting around and waiting for life to come to you probably won't work at all well, whereas grabbing the bull by the horns can help you to get you what you want. There's always a possibility that things might go slightly wrong, but risk-taking is your business.

9 SUNDAY
Moon Age Day 2   Moon Sign Aries

am . . . .

pm . . . .
It's still worth getting involved and making the most of any opportunity that comes your way. In amongst a busy schedule you ought to find time to listen to what your partner is saying. You may not always give enough attention to your romantic life, but if you put aside a little time to do so now, the results could be rewarding.

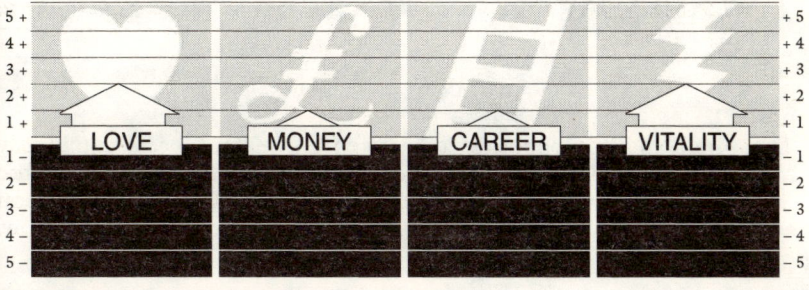

10 MONDAY

Moon Age Day 3   Moon Sign Aries

am . . . .

pm . . . .
This is hardly the best time of the month to be overconfident or to expect situations to come good of their own accord. Actually you will have to put in a good deal more effort than normal if you want to get ahead, and you could find colleagues or friends slightly less helpful than they may have seemed to be of late.

11 TUESDAY

Moon Age Day 4   Moon Sign Taurus

am . . . .

pm . . . .
Even if practicalities are going slightly wrong, your love life is particularly favoured. With strong supporting planetary influences it looks as though you will be well able to make the most favourable of impressions – either on your existing partner or in the direction of someone you wish was the love of your life.

12 WEDNESDAY

Moon Age Day 5   Moon Sign Taurus

am . . . .

pm . . . .
Give yourself a brief pat on the back for any success you achieve early today, but don't get too overconfident because there is more to be done. You can afford to be very progressive in your attitude today, particularly towards work, but there are some slightly less favourable moments to come and you need to show caution.

13 THURSDAY

Moon Age Day 6   Moon Sign Gemini

am . . . .

pm . . . .
The Moon in your opposite zodiac sign encourages a less confident, more cautious and altogether quieter Archer than would usually be the case. There is no inference that things will go wrong, but if you lack your accustomed belief in yourself you could be quieter and less responsive to opportunities.

14 FRIDAY
Moon Age Day 7   Moon Sign Gemini

am . . . .

pm . . . .
Keep it casual and personal today and can't really go too far wrong. This is probably not the best time of the month to be thinking about major alterations to your working life and nor are you likely to be at your most energetic. It's worth spending some time in the company of people who please you just by being around.

15 SATURDAY
Moon Age Day 8   Moon Sign Cancer

am . . . .

pm . . . .
Just a few hours away from the lunar low and already you have scope to improve things. It shouldn't be half as hard today to see your way forward – or to convince other people that you know what you are talking about, even if you don't. You can now be the master of your own destiny, which is the way the Archer likes life to be.

16 SUNDAY
Moon Age Day 9   Moon Sign Cancer

am . . . .

pm . . . .
With strong planetary influences pushing from behind, you can now capitalise on some of the most positive trends of the month. What is most valuable is your charm, which you can put to good use in a social sense. This might not be the best day of the week for making professional progress but you can at least let your hair down.

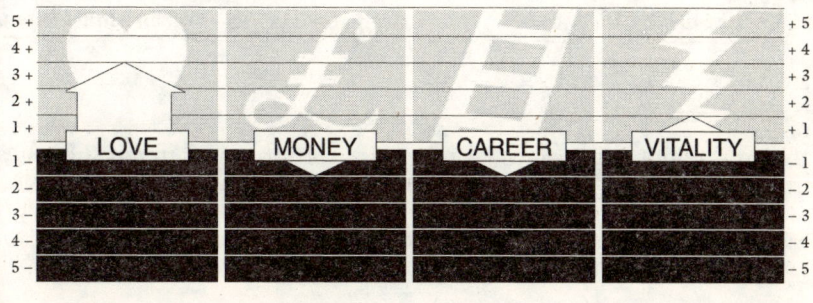

17 MONDAY *Moon Age Day 10* *Moon Sign Cancer*

am . . . .

pm . . . .
The Moon in the zodiac sign of Cancer encourages you to show a more sensitive side to your nature, though there are also influences about that could push you in the direction of showing a more aggressive side to your nature in professional settings. One thing is for certain – you shouldn't be easily fooled today.

18 TUESDAY *Moon Age Day 11* *Moon Sign Leo*

am . . . .

pm . . . .
Dynamic at work and a pussycat at home, that's what works best for Sagittarius at the moment. Look out for anything inspirational and take any opportunity to feed the more refined side of your nature. The Archer is a true intellectual at present and you can afford to revel in cultured and beautiful surroundings.

19 WEDNESDAY *Moon Age Day 12* *Moon Sign Leo*

am . . . .

pm . . . .
Anything someone else can do, you can do better – or at least that's the way you may feel around this time. Be careful though, because pride goes before a fall and you could just discover that you are not quite as capable as you thought. This would be particularly true on those occasions when you know you are out of your depth.

20 THURSDAY *Moon Age Day 13* *Moon Sign Virgo*

am . . . .

pm . . . .
If your intuition tells you to take a specific sort of action, trends suggest that you should be listening to its advice. You now have what it takes to see clear through to the heart of just about any matter and you shouldn't easily be duped or sent off at a tangent. Be prepared to find out what is going on and then arrange your life carefully.

21 FRIDAY
Moon Age Day 14   Moon Sign Virgo

am . . . .

pm . . . .
You have the ability to remain very much in charge of most situations, but there could be moments in your personal life that will be more difficult to negotiate. Make sure that you spend enough time, attention and money in making your lover feel really wanted. In this way you can defuse a situation before it becomes a real issue.

22 SATURDAY
Moon Age Day 15   Moon Sign Libra

am . . . .

pm . . . .
You may be very keen to get new plans underway this weekend but might be restricted if those around you are not as organised as you seem to be. The time could be right to go it alone or at least to threaten to do so. That should soon make people sit up and take notice. Younger family members might be irritating you.

23 SUNDAY
Moon Age Day 16   Moon Sign Libra

am . . . .

pm . . . .
Today should be better, particularly if you make your own position abundantly clear and don't accept any nonsense. Showing others that the Archer means business would be no bad thing. As a rule you are a very easy-going sort of person but your Fire-sign credentials can be displayed from time to time.

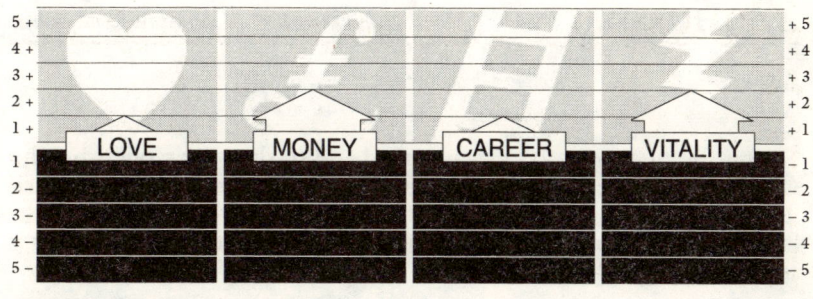

24 MONDAY   *Moon Age Day 17   Moon Sign Libra*

am . . . .

pm . . . .
You would be wise to retain a sense of purpose and determination as a new working week gets started. There won't be a better time during March to get something new started or to travel. It doesn't matter how short or long a potential journey might be, it's the change it brings and the possibilities that it presents that prove to be important.

25 TUESDAY   *Moon Age Day 18   Moon Sign Scorpio*

am . . . .

pm . . . .
It's possible that someone might accuse you of being odd or even downright peculiar today and it has to be said that compared to some individuals, you are. The Archer is unique, if only because it refuses to stick to convention and tends to make its mind up on the spur of the moment. Nothing could suit you better under present trends.

26 WEDNESDAY   *Moon Age Day 19   Moon Sign Scorpio*

am . . . .

pm . . . .
A potentially quieter day today, as the Moon sits in your solar twelfth house. You can still show a fairly unique attitude towards life, though in a less obvious way for the moment. With the lunar high coming along tomorrow this might prove to be a good time to clear the decks for action. Gambling wouldn't be wise now.

27 THURSDAY   *Moon Age Day 20   Moon Sign Sagittarius*

am . . . .

pm . . . .
Now is the right time to take command and to show everyone what the Archer can achieve when it really tries. Be prepared to use the good luck that is available, simply be what you naturally are when at your best. People should love to have you around because you are intelligent, funny and excellent company.

28 FRIDAY
Moon Age Day 21   *Moon Sign Sagittarius*

am . . . .

pm . . . .

News, views and quite definite opinions – that's what you can give to others at the moment. Your stimulated mind won't be still for a minute and you can use every minute to further your own ends and those of the people you love. It's amazing just how much one person can get done in a single day!

29 SATURDAY
Moon Age Day 22   *Moon Sign Sagittarius*

am . . . .

pm . . . .

This would be an excellent time for marshalling your energies into one specific project. If you are too quick on the uptake you may leave everyone else behind, so it's worth listening to what friends have to say. You may not act on their advice but at least you will be better informed, and that can really count at the moment.

30 SUNDAY
Moon Age Day 23   *Moon Sign Capricorn*

am . . . .

pm . . . .

This might well be the first time so far this year that you have really taken notice of the changing seasons. If you are not working today you may decide to get out into the good fresh air – preferably alongside someone you love to be with. Country or coast, it doesn't matter because it's the change of scene that counts.

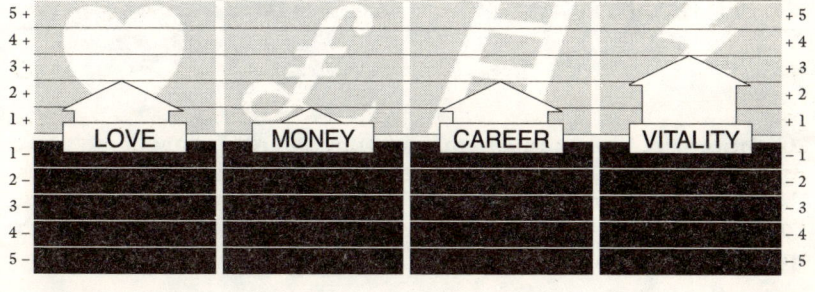

31 MONDAY *Moon Age Day 24 Moon Sign Capricorn*

am . . . .

pm . . . .
With a new working week in view and everything to play for, the Archer can afford to be just about as positive as can be. Not everything might work out quite the way you might expect, but you are the best person in the world at thinking on your feet. What is more, you can make gains when life is unpredictable.

1 TUESDAY *Moon Age Day 25 Moon Sign Aquarius*

am . . . .

pm . . . .
There isn't really much chance of you being an April Fool today, that is unless you choose to put yourself in that position. Anyone trying to dupe you would have to get up very early in the day, though you may well decide to show a definite kindness and allow yourself to be the centre of a joke or two, simply to please those around you.

2 WEDNESDAY *Moon Age Day 26 Moon Sign Aquarius*

am . . . .

pm . . . .
Your mind needs constant stimulation, which is why you rarely do the same thing for more than ten minutes at a time. However, the support of both Mercury and Mars presently makes it easier for you to concentrate, which is why today would be excellent for making certain that something very important is finally put to bed.

3 THURSDAY *Moon Age Day 27 Moon Sign Pisces*

am . . . .

pm . . . .
Get-togethers can be made both interesting and rewarding, in more than one way. If there is something on your mind that can only be sorted out by an expert, this could be the best time of the month to approach one. It might cost you money, but a problem that could get worse with the passing of time can be solved.

4 FRIDAY   *Moon Age Day 28   Moon Sign Pisces*

am . . . .

pm . . . .
Trends suggest that following tried and tested paths is not your best option today. Instead, it's worth doing things in your own way. This may not please everyone but innovation is your middle name and if nobody ever tried out alternatives, life would stand still. If you are in the mood to be original, who in the world can stop you?

5 SATURDAY   *Moon Age Day 29 · Moon Sign Pisces*

am . . . .

pm . . . .
This could turn out to be a weekend of definite contrasts. Things could get boring if you stick around at home, or if you do things the way you do almost every weekend. On the other hand you can enjoy some genuine excitement, simply by ringing the changes. There isn't much doubt about which option you will embrace.

6 SUNDAY   *Moon Age Day 0   Moon Sign Aries*

am . . . .

pm . . . .
Now is the time to stand up for friends and relatives and show the world just how courageous the Archer can be. Actually you may not have to try too hard if you show others that you mean business. Set your feet, look sternly at those who try to be awkward and then turn away and smile.

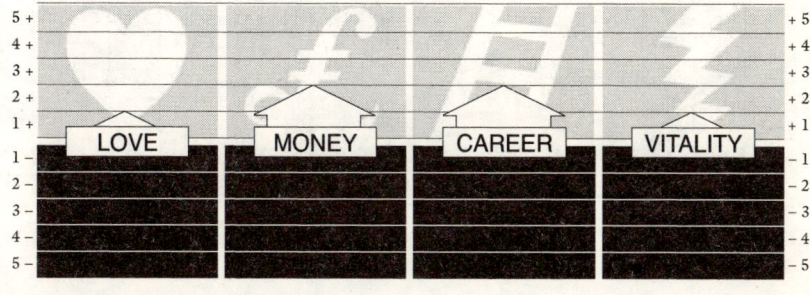

April 2008

YOUR MONTH AT A GLANCE

⊕ = Opportunities are around   ⊖ = Be on the defensive   ⬤ = Life is pretty ordinary

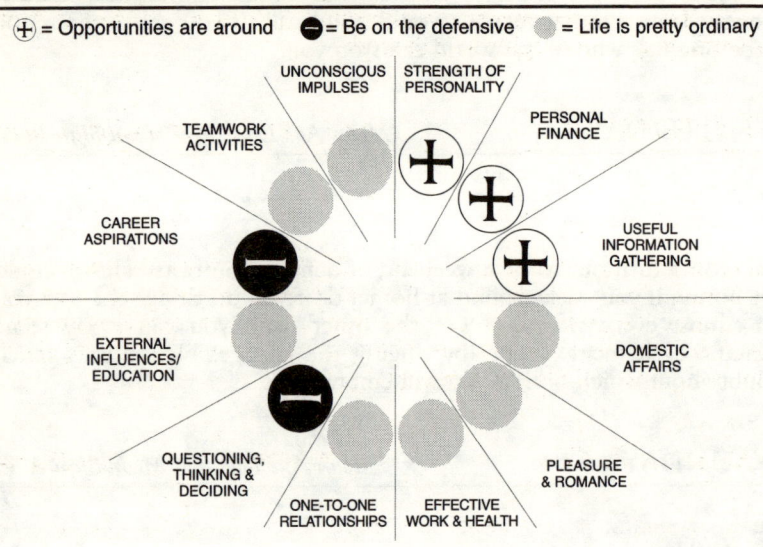

UNCONSCIOUS IMPULSES

STRENGTH OF PERSONALITY

TEAMWORK ACTIVITIES

PERSONAL FINANCE

CAREER ASPIRATIONS

USEFUL INFORMATION GATHERING

EXTERNAL INFLUENCES/ EDUCATION

DOMESTIC AFFAIRS

QUESTIONING, THINKING & DECIDING

PLEASURE & ROMANCE

ONE-TO-ONE RELATIONSHIPS

EFFECTIVE WORK & HEALTH

APRIL HIGHS AND LOWS

Here I show you how the rhythms of the Moon will affect you this month. Like the tide, your energies and abilities will rise and fall with its pattern. When it is above the centre line, go for it, when it is below, you should be resting.

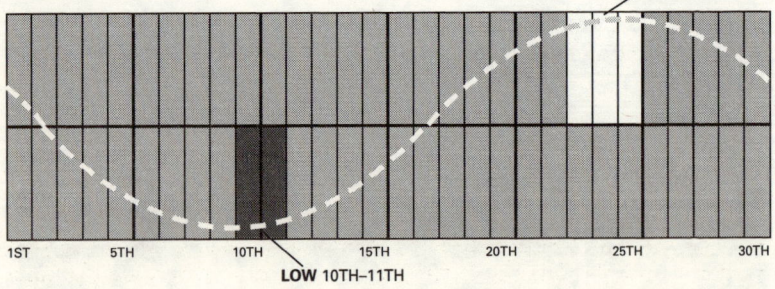

HIGH 23RD–25TH

LOW 10TH–11TH

1ST   5TH   10TH   15TH   20TH   25TH   30TH

7 MONDAY   *Moon Age Day 1   Moon Sign Aries*

am . . . .

pm . . . .
It is around this time that old situations begin to break down and some
of them will have be to rebuilt in a new way. This is not a situation that
need worry you much at all because the Archer is always committed to
change. If you use the energy that is around, at least for the first part of
this week, you can plough through work.

8 TUESDAY   *Moon Age Day 2   Moon Sign Taurus*

am . . . .

pm . . . .
You can best avoid tense situations by actively employing the funny side
of your nature. You can be the most humorous person around when the
mood takes you and this is a sure-fire way to defuse potential problems.
Not everyone responds to your charm at the moment, particularly if
there is a degree of jealousy involved.

9 WEDNESDAY   *Moon Age Day 3   Moon Sign Taurus*

am . . . .

pm . . . .
Your intuition is very strong and will guide you wisely if you allow it to
do so. This does mean that you may have to spend just a little time
weighing up the pros and cons of certain situations, but the wait should
be more than worthwhile. Stand to make the most of a positive interlude
as far as your love life is concerned.

10 THURSDAY   *Moon Age Day 4   Moon Sign Gemini*

am . . . .

pm . . . .
You want to get on and do things, but influences don't help you to make
the progress you are certain is possible. Welcome to the lunar low for
April. The best way forward is to stay still for a couple of days. Instead of
getting frustrated about the situation, use this time wisely by planning
and organising.

11 FRIDAY

Moon Age Day 5   Moon Sign Gemini

am . . . .

pm . . . .
Things may still be rather quiet, and you may decide that the best way to deal with life is to batter your way through situations. Nothing could be further from the truth because you will be up against irremovable objects. Why not let others do the grafting, whilst you call in a few favours that have been owing to you for some time?

12 SATURDAY

Moon Age Day 6   Moon Sign Cancer

am . . . .

pm . . . .
You can now get things moving in your direction again, using a weekend of new opportunities and a greater involvement with both family members and much-valued friends. The restrictions are lifted and this means you could be somewhat spoiled for choice when it comes to deciding what you should do next.

13 SUNDAY

Moon Age Day 7   Moon Sign Cancer

am . . . .

pm . . . .
If it's difficult to find help today, you may have to do things yourself that you had relied on others to complete for you. This is a minor inconvenience and is not worth making a fuss about. By the time you have spoken your mind you could have done the job five times over. Stay calm and cool today.

	LOVE	MONEY	CAREER	VITALITY	
5 +					+ 5
4 +					+ 4
3 +					+ 3
2 +					+ 2
1 +					+ 1
1 -					- 1
2 -					- 2
3 -					- 3
4 -					- 4
5 -					- 5

14 MONDAY   *Moon Age Day 8   Moon Sign Leo*

am . . . .

pm . . . .
There are planetary influences around now that could offer you a short
period of significant inner reflection. The Archer is often on the go and
you rarely get the moments of calm and reflection that you need. Today
could be an exception, particularly if you are willing to stand and watch
the flowers grow.

15 TUESDAY   *Moon Age Day 9   Moon Sign Leo*

am . . . .

pm . . . .
Even if you are still somewhat more reflective than normal, this needn't
prevent you from making progress in a number of different ways. Today
offers you scope to get the measure of adversaries or outright
competitors, and you could be particularly successful in any sort of
sporting activity you may take on. Good luck is on offer at present.

16 WEDNESDAY   *Moon Age Day 10   Moon Sign Virgo*

am . . . .

pm . . . .
Trust your hunches and you can go far, though if you constantly question
yourself and your own motives there are sticking points ahead. This
would certainly be the best day of the week for travel, and any journey
that is taken more or less on the spur of the moment can prove to be
particularly useful and enjoyable.

17 THURSDAY   *Moon Age Day 11   Moon Sign Virgo*

am . . . .

pm . . . .
Impatience needs to be curbed at present because it could cause you to
do things wrongly or with less panache than is normally the case. There
are moments when you need to stand back from life and look on in a
detached manner. This may only take a few moments but it could prove
to be worthwhile in helping you to avoid making mistakes.

18 FRIDAY

Moon Age Day 12   Moon Sign Libra

am . . . .

pm . . . .
Persuading others that you have what it takes to succeed can help you to
gain allies now. Sagittarius is on a roll, and looks especially attractive to
the world at large. Compliments could well be coming in thick and fast.
One or two of them might even be slightly embarrassing.

19 SATURDAY

Moon Age Day 13   Moon Sign Libra

am . . . .

pm . . . .
The greatest contentment to be found today comes from being in the
company of people you both like and respect. Once the responsibilities
of the day are dealt with you can afford to look for ways to have fun, and
if you are not in the right frame of mind to go it alone, you may decide
to enlist the support of friends.

20 SUNDAY

Moon Age Day 14   Moon Sign Libra

am . . . .

pm . . . .
Conversations with loved ones can help you to make new starts at home,
and some Archers might even be thinking about quite dramatic changes
in the weeks ahead. It's worth talking to family members because
planetary trends show this to be the best period during April to put a past
argument behind you and to strengthen blood ties.

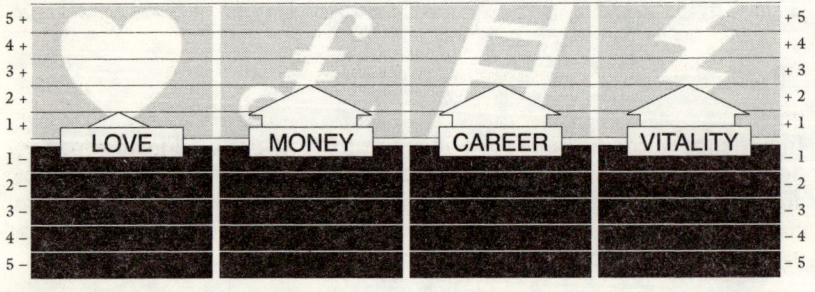

21 MONDAY
Moon Age Day 15   Moon Sign Scorpio

am . . . .

pm . . . .
You could take advantage of a very quiet start to the new working week because as the Moon passes through your solar twelfth house you are encouraged to meditate and look on, rather than take part in everything as a matter of course. Today is ideal for catching up with written communication.

22 TUESDAY
Moon Age Day 16   Moon Sign Scorpio

am . . . .

pm . . . .
Don't push your luck for the moment, even if it seems that you have everything it takes to get ahead. There is plenty of opportunity to be dynamic over the next three days, and for the moment you can achieve much more by looking and planning ahead. It's worth seeking support and entertainment from friends.

23 WEDNESDAY
Moon Age Day 17   Moon Sign Sagittarius

am . . . .

pm . . . .
With the lunar high comes a greater opportunity than ever to get ahead of the pack. If you co-operate at all today it can be from a position of power and influence, because you needn't play second fiddle to anyone. All the same you can achieve your ends with so much kindness and charm that people will be glad to see you succeed.

24 THURSDAY
Moon Age Day 18   Moon Sign Sagittarius

am . . . .

pm . . . .
It looks as though you are definitely on a roll now when it comes to getting what you want from life in a material sense. Personal matters are less well defined, probably because you simply don't have the time to stand and talk. Routines would get on your nerves today, so be prepared to be as fresh and original as proves to be possible.

25 FRIDAY
Moon Age Day 19   Moon Sign Sagittarius

am . . . .

pm . . . .
Lady Luck is still available to help you, so you can afford to continue chancing your arm. There's nothing new about this because it is the way you live your life most of the time, but what is different is that it seems you cannot put a foot wrong. As the day wears on you can make the most of your creative potential.

26 SATURDAY
Moon Age Day 20   Moon Sign Capricorn

am . . . .

pm . . . .
You may not get on too well today with people who insist on being awkward or disruptive. It's fine for you to do almost anything that takes your fancy, but you don't always approve of other people throwing a spanner in the works. If the Archer does have a fault it is that you can be rather selfish on occasions – something to work on.

27 SUNDAY
Moon Age Day 21   Moon Sign Capricorn

am . . . .

pm . . . .
You would be wise to avoid heated discussions or arguments today because you really don't need them at the moment. You get on best when left alone to do things in your own way, or when you are alongside people with whom you have always felt very comfortable. If you are forced into a row today, you could be quite cutting.

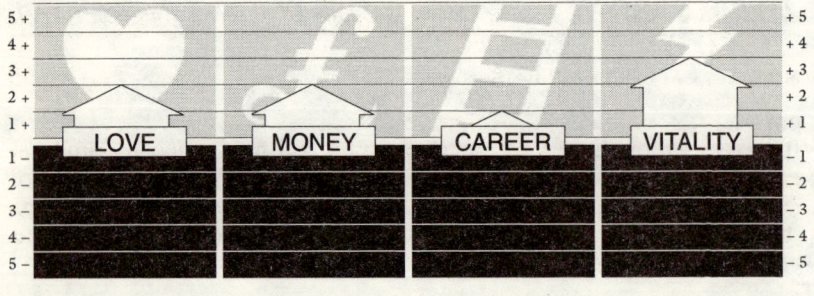

28 MONDAY
Moon Age Day 22   Moon Sign Aquarius

am . . . .

pm . . . .
Sagittarius is a very idealistic zodiac sign but your real saving grace is your ability to bend with the wind. That's going to be especially important this week, particularly if some of your most cherished hopes for the future receive setbacks. What does that matter to you? It's simply a case of thinking up something even more exciting.

29 TUESDAY
Moon Age Day 23   Moon Sign Aquarius

am . . . .

pm . . . .
Your strength lies in remaining optimistic and open-minded in your general attitude to life. This might not win you any prizes but it could get you a new friend or two. The people who really matter to you at present are those who have stuck by you through thick and thin. Spending some quality time with your partner would be no bad thing.

30 WEDNESDAY
Moon Age Day 24   Moon Sign Aquarius

am . . . .

pm . . . .
You can strengthen your finances by making the most of your earning potential. You might have to speculate a little in order to accumulate but you can be both shrewd and calculating at the moment. On a more personal note you need to make your feelings abundantly clear to get the best from romance.

1 THURSDAY
Moon Age Day 25   Moon Sign Pisces

am . . . .

pm . . . .
A new month dawns and May offers scope for you to move even closer to achieving some of those longed-for objectives. You can best deal with any delays and disruptions by seeing them as nothing more than temporary issues that you can solve. Your sensible attitude helps you to win admirers, not least amongst superiors.

2 FRIDAY
Moon Age Day 26   Moon Sign Pisces

am . . . .

pm . . . .
Trends still assist you to shine when in public situations, even on those rare occasions when you are shaking like a jelly inside. Your ability to give the impression that you are cool, calm and relaxed is a great help at the moment. In social settings a little cheek can go a long way and can get you somewhere very interesting.

3 SATURDAY
Moon Age Day 27   Moon Sign Aries

am . . . .

pm . . . .
Joint ventures work well for you, as is usually the case for Sagittarius, but you may not be getting on with everyone. In particular you might have little patience with individuals you see as being self-centred. Your nature is very idealistic at the moment and you may well decide to speak your mind – even when it would be better not to.

4 SUNDAY
Moon Age Day 28   Moon Sign Aries

am . . . .

pm . . . .
By all means stand up for your rights and for those of people who are less dynamic and self-assured than you are, but exercise a little caution all the same. There is no point in flying off the handle about issues you haven't first looked at carefully. If you are too impetuous you could end up regretting the fact and having to apologise.

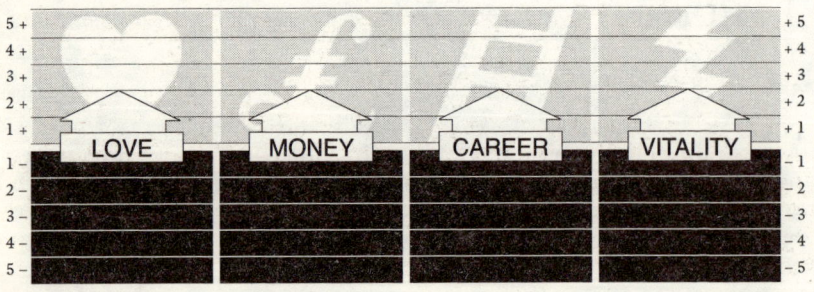

May
2008

YOUR MONTH AT A GLANCE

⊕ = Opportunities are around ⊖ = Be on the defensive ○ = Life is pretty ordinary

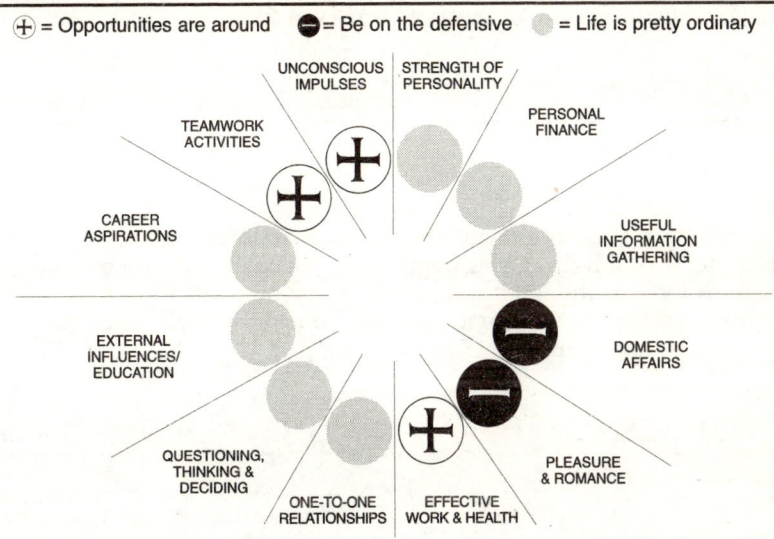

UNCONSCIOUS IMPULSES

STRENGTH OF PERSONALITY

PERSONAL FINANCE

TEAMWORK ACTIVITIES

CAREER ASPIRATIONS

USEFUL INFORMATION GATHERING

EXTERNAL INFLUENCES/ EDUCATION

DOMESTIC AFFAIRS

QUESTIONING, THINKING & DECIDING

ONE-TO-ONE RELATIONSHIPS

EFFECTIVE WORK & HEALTH

PLEASURE & ROMANCE

MAY HIGHS AND LOWS

Here I show you how the rhythms of the Moon will affect you this month. Like the tide, your energies and abilities will rise and fall with its pattern. When it is above the centre line, go for it, when it is below, you should be resting.

HIGH 21ST–22ND

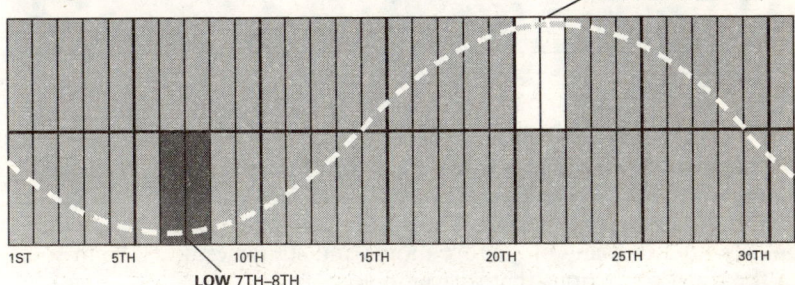

1ST   5TH   10TH   15TH   20TH   25TH   30TH

LOW 7TH–8TH

5 MONDAY
Moon Age Day 0   Moon Sign Taurus

am . . . .

pm . . . .
The focus is on dealing with problems today, especially those caused by others. Younger family members in particular may be taxing your patience and your ingenuity, but on the whole you can ensure that there is a very humorous side to most of what takes place.

6 TUESDAY
Moon Age Day 1   Moon Sign Taurus

am . . . .

pm . . . .
You can make Tuesday a slightly better day, even if you still aren't getting on quite as positively as you might wish, especially in the professional stakes. It looks as though it will be Friday before trends allow substantial progress, and in the meantime you need to address small issues that are nevertheless important.

7 WEDNESDAY
Moon Age Day 2   Moon Sign Gemini

am . . . .

pm . . . .
With the lunar low comes not only the potentially quietest period in May but also the one that paradoxically should cause you the least stress or worry. You may not be getting on very fast, but neither will you be too bothered about the fact. This may well be the best chance for relaxation that the Archer gets in May – so employ it.

8 THURSDAY
Moon Age Day 3   Moon Sign Gemini

am . . . .

pm . . . .
A day when slowing things down helps you to see through all situations extremely clearly. For everyone else life seems normal but to you it's like seeing things in slow motion. The great advantage here is that you have endless time to plan your future moves and strategies, freed from some of the usual restrictions that surround you.

9 FRIDAY

Moon Age Day 4   Moon Sign Cancer

am . . . .

pm . . . .
Now you have a chance to put some of your planning into action and, with the lunar low out of the way, to speed up life significantly. Still, it's been a good time to recharge your batteries and with busy times ahead you will probably be glad you had the chance.

10 SATURDAY

Moon Age Day 5   Moon Sign Cancer

am . . . .

pm . . . .
You needn't settle for a weekend of absolute normality. If you are really to spark off your mind you need to do different things, maybe in the company of people who don't figure in your life very much. Today is not a time to get tied down by routines, and you get on far better when left alone to run your own destiny.

11 SUNDAY

Moon Age Day 6   Moon Sign Leo

am . . . .

pm . . . .
You can afford to be fairly happy with your lot today and to show a happy face to the world at large. An ideal day to find pleasure in the achievements and plans of family and friends. Don't get unnecessarily jealous about something really silly.

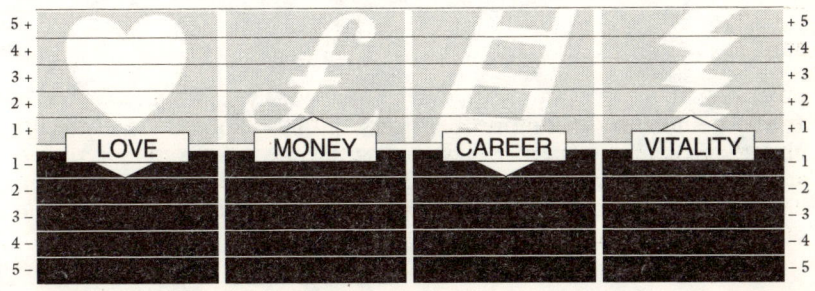

12 MONDAY
Moon Age Day 7   Moon Sign Leo

am . . . .

pm . . . .
With the start of a new working week comes a day or two of quite intense responsibility. This needn't worry you in the slightest because stress doesn't really figure in your life just at the moment. You have what it takes to offer timely support to those around you.

13 TUESDAY
Moon Age Day 8   Moon Sign Virgo

am . . . .

pm . . . .
Rewards are there for the taking for Archers who are willing to suspend belief and try something completely new and possibly quite revolutionary. You are never one to stand still and just at the moment the pace you manage to maintain can mystify slower types. You have what it takes to turn heads in most social situations.

14 WEDNESDAY
Moon Age Day 9   Moon Sign Virgo

am . . . .

pm . . . .
Keep up the pressure to change situations to your advantage. Not everyone might find you to be absolutely attractive today and you could come across one or two people who definitely don't like you at all. This is not something to dwell on, because no matter how hard you try, you can't please everyone all of the time.

15 THURSDAY
Moon Age Day 10   Moon Sign Virgo

am . . . .

pm . . . .
It may be time to think more about relationships at home and especially about your romantic partner. Being a Sagittarian you are often on the go and may not always give as much thought to your lover as you might. The opportunity to redress that balance slightly comes along today, and you should not miss it.

16 FRIDAY   *Moon Age Day 11   Moon Sign Libra*

am . . . .

pm . . . .
Trends now enhance your ability to deal with people who are down in the dumps. Not only do you have what it takes to cheer them up but you are also filled with practical suggestions as to how they can make their own lives better. Just be careful you don't end up being accused of interfering!

17 SATURDAY   *Moon Age Day 12   Moon Sign Libra*

am . . . .

pm . . . .
Saturday brings a chance to get out there, and if retail therapy is on your mind this could be the best day of May to go shopping. There are bargains to be had but in order to get the best from them you will need to be slightly discriminating. Persuading friends to tag along could be the recipe for lots of fun.

18 SUNDAY   *Moon Age Day 13   Moon Sign Scorpio*

am . . . .

pm . . . .
The year is advancing fast and things are starting to bloom in the garden and the local parks. This could be a good time to go out and look at nature. You are now in the mood for refined pastimes and interludes. With a twelfth-house Moon in place you could also be rather more contemplative and slightly less pushy than usual.

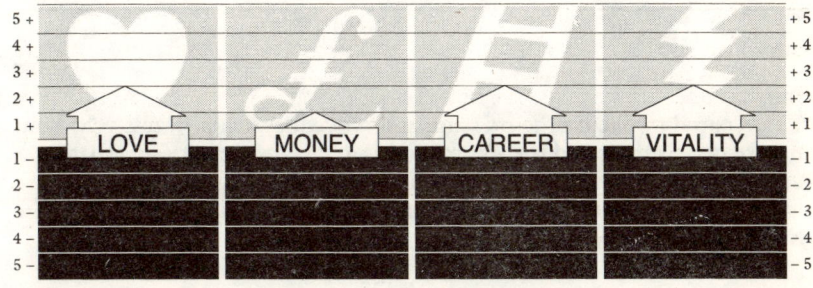

19 MONDAY

Moon Age Day 14   Moon Sign Scorpio

am . . . .

pm . . . .
The time is right to give yourself a pat on the back for something that has come good after weeks or months of hard work, and perhaps take a short break before you pitch in again. Yours is a life that rarely stands still but you can afford to take the odd moment for reflection. Helping others is also favoured.

20 TUESDAY

Moon Age Day 15   Moon Sign Scorpio

am . . . .

pm . . . .
If some of your efforts have ground to a halt for the moment, your best approach is to wait. You will be sensible enough to realise that misplaced energy is usually wasted, which is why you should be quite happy today to bide your time. By tomorrow everything could look very different.

21 WEDNESDAY

Moon Age Day 16   Moon Sign Sagittarius

am . . . .

pm . . . .
The Moon returns to your zodiac sign and with it come some of the best incentives you will encounter during May. There is strong support from planets other than the Moon and your most likely sphere of influence at present is through your work. Why not use this time to let people know what you think?

22 THURSDAY

Moon Age Day 17   Moon Sign Sagittarius

am . . . .

pm . . . .
Be prepared to pile on the pressure and move forward progressively. Your nature is charming and the impression you give in almost any situation is certainly going to do you good. With such a bright twinkle in your eye and in possession of limitless charm, you can also make this one of the most important romantic times.

23 FRIDAY
Moon Age Day 18   Moon Sign Capricorn

am . . . .

pm . . . .
If standard responses don't work today, you are going to have to think of new and ingenious strategies if you really want to get on. Beware of spending money unless you are certain it is going to work for you. Otherwise you should keep your purse strings firmly tied whilst you wait for a more advantageous time.

24 SATURDAY
Moon Age Day 19   Moon Sign Capricorn

am . . . .

pm . . . .
Financial caution is still favoured, though that doesn't really matter because the things that bring you the greatest happiness at the moment come absolutely free of charge. Spending time with your lover or with family members could well be number one on your agenda today.

25 SUNDAY
Moon Age Day 20   Moon Sign Capricorn

am . . . .

pm . . . .
Now you have more scope to act on impulse, especially when it comes to speaking your mind. That's fine as far as it goes but there are occasions on which you could say too much – or the right thing to the wrong person. You need to be totally in charge of your mouth at the moment, and that usually means thinking before you speak.

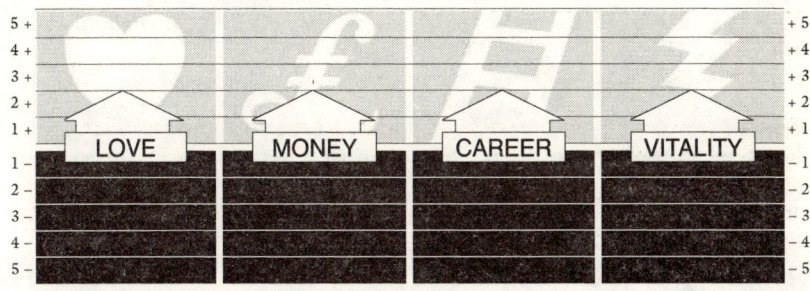

26 MONDAY
Moon Age Day 21   Moon Sign Aquarius

am . . . .

pm . . . .
Be prepared to be active and enterprising, despite mixed financial trends.
You have scope to strengthen your finances, though you might have to
wait a few days to reap the benefits. In the meantime you need to curb
your enthusiasm for spending and to call in a few debts if you haven't
done so already.

27 TUESDAY ☿
Moon Age Day 22   Moon Sign Aquarius

am . . . .

pm . . . .
Planetary trends now favour social interaction and the ability to get
together with fascinating and even stimulating sorts of people. Romance
looks good and for those Archers who have been seeking a new love, now
is one of those times when you should be looking. Help yourself by
getting together with like-minded people.

28 WEDNESDAY ☿
Moon Age Day 23   Moon Sign Pisces

am . . . .

pm . . . .
You can best avoid the midweek blues by doing something completely
different and by taking along someone of whom you are fond. Avoid
noisy or vexatious types at the moment and certainly don't get involved
in heated discussions or arguments. There is a calm and serenity just
below the surface and it's up to you to find it.

29 THURSDAY ☿
Moon Age Day 24   Moon Sign Pisces

am . . . .

pm . . . .
You have scope to turn the tide in favour of greater financial success and
gain, though it might not seem that way at first today. Get your thinking
cap on because there are definitely ways in which you can help yourself at
the moment. In addition you could enlist the support of someone who
is in the know regarding money.

30 FRIDAY   ☿   *Moon Age Day 25*   *Moon Sign Aries*

am . . . .

pm . . . .
You have a right to speak up if you think you are being put upon today, though you may actively choose to take the rough with the smooth in terms of jobs you don't really like. This can help you prove to the world that you won't instruct anyone to undertake tasks you are unwilling to have a go at yourself. Bravo for the Archer!

31 SATURDAY   ☿   *Moon Age Day 26*   *Moon Sign Aries*

am . . . .

pm . . . .
There is no room at the moment to be too satisfied with your own actions or opinions. You can always learn something, and adopting an attitude that says you are always correct is not going to help at all. A little humility goes a long way, particularly to the Archer. And even if you're not humble, you could at least pretend to be.

1 SUNDAY   ☿   *Moon Age Day 27*   *Moon Sign Taurus*

am . . . .

pm . . . .
There is a strong possibility of extraordinary coincidences and unusual happenings today, which should certainly make you sit up and take notice. It's as if life itself is offering you signposts for the future. What matters is that you read these correctly and adopt the right attitude to benefit from all that could be on offer.

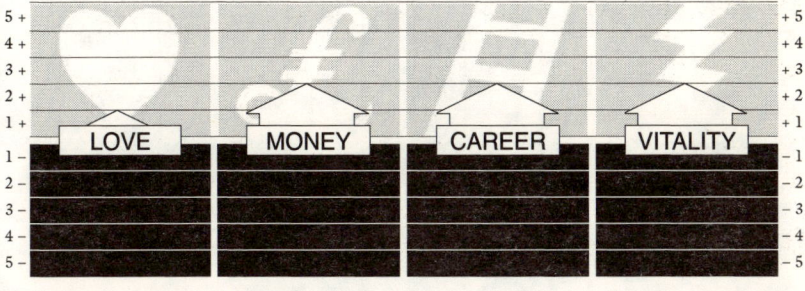

June 2008

YOUR MONTH AT A GLANCE

⊕ = Opportunities are around   ⊖ = Be on the defensive   ⬤ = Life is pretty ordinary

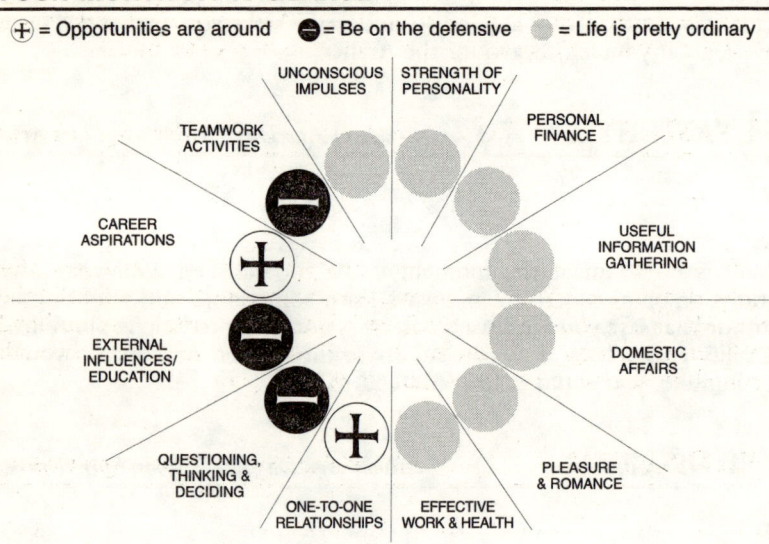

JUNE HIGHS AND LOWS

Here I show you how the rhythms of the Moon will affect you this month. Like the tide, your energies and abilities will rise and fall with its pattern. When it is above the centre line, go for it, when it is below, you should be resting.

HIGH 17TH–18TH

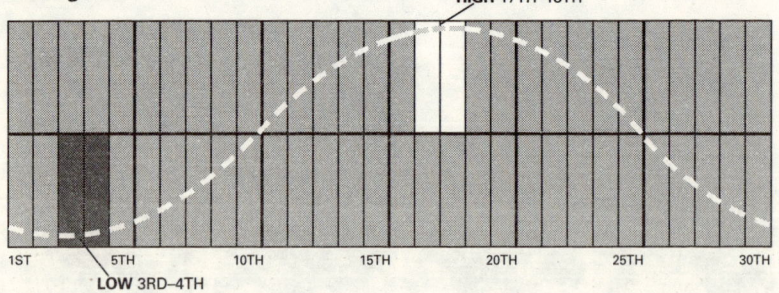

LOW 3RD–4TH

2 MONDAY ☿ *Moon Age Day 28* *Moon Sign Taurus*

am . . . .

pm . . . .
How wonderful life can now seem to the average Sagittarian, though not if you spend all your time today worrying and fussing over matters that are not at all important. Your best approach is to keep an eye on the main chance and learn all you can about progress. Maybe you could take a leaf out of the book of a colleague – even one you don't like much.

3 TUESDAY ☿ *Moon Age Day 29* *Moon Sign Gemini*

am . . . .

pm . . . .
Another slower interlude is now possible, though the lunar low this month has the sting taken out of its tail by a very positive position of the planet Mars in your solar chart. Whilst it is usually sensible to stand and wait when the Moon is in Gemini, this time around you can get through or round most obstacles that are strewn in your path.

4 WEDNESDAY ☿ *Moon Age Day 0* *Moon Sign Gemini*

am . . . .

pm . . . .
Try not to be too impulsive for the moment and take what life offers without grumbling too much. If you are being watched at the moment, the way you deal with little irritations is important. What might be harder than keeping yourself on the move today will be shifting a colleague or friend who is a reincarnated tortoise!

5 THURSDAY ☿ *Moon Age Day 1* *Moon Sign Cancer*

am . . . .

pm . . . .
Standard responses may not work today and you might have to get your thinking cap on in order to make things go the way you wish. This won't come about by forcing issues but rather by employing a little psychology. Even if you persuade friends to follow your lead, your partner could be less willing.

6 FRIDAY ☿ *Moon Age Day 2   Moon Sign Cancer*

am . . . .

pm . . . .
If you are in too much of a hurry to complete a specific project today, that could mean getting things wrong. Better by far to watch and listen, because the things others are doing and saying can prove to be very informative. This would be a fine time to think about taking a journey – even one arranged at the last minute.

7 SATURDAY ☿ *Moon Age Day 3   Moon Sign Leo*

am . . . .

pm . . . .
As far as life in general is concerned this weekend should offer you a potential winning streak. It isn't necessarily that anything major is going your way, simply that you can feel fairly good about most aspects of your life. The more optimistic you are, the better are the prospects for both today and tomorrow.

8 SUNDAY ☿ *Moon Age Day 4   Moon Sign Leo*

am . . . .

pm . . . .
A day to capitalise on highlights in relationship issues, and to try to get away from routines. An early vacation might appeal but if you can't ring the changes by going on holiday you could at least decide to make alterations to your home or garden. What matters now is any sort of stimulation.

	LOVE	MONEY	CAREER	VITALITY
5 +				+ 5
4 +				+ 4
3 +				+ 3
2 +				+ 2
1 +				+ 1
1 -				- 1
2 -				- 2
3 -				- 3
4 -				- 4
5 -				- 5

9 MONDAY ☿ *Moon Age Day 5* *Moon Sign Leo*

am . . . .

pm . . . .
You may well be rather too volatile for your own good at the start of this particular working week, especially if colleagues seem to be behaving in a particularly inept or stupid way. Your best approach is to calm down a little and take things more in your stride. The greater your self-control at the moment, the more you can get on with others.

10 TUESDAY ☿ *Moon Age Day 6* *Moon Sign Virgo*

am . . . .

pm . . . .
Rather than flying off the handle today, it's worth trying to slow down somewhat. The Moon has now entered Virgo, and this time around that could support a slightly more introspective quality for a couple of days. However this is by no means certain for all Sagittarians.

11 WEDNESDAY ☿ *Moon Age Day 7* *Moon Sign Virgo*

am . . . .

pm . . . .
Don't be too quick to judge either people or situations right now, because some things are not at all what they first appear to be. The best way to deal with life today is to turn your intuition up to full volume, whilst at the same time employing that Fire-sign common sense that so rarely lets you down. That's a combination that works well.

12 THURSDAY ☿ *Moon Age Day 8* *Moon Sign Libra*

am . . . .

pm . . . .
Use your creative and inspirational potential to increase your popularity with both colleagues and people you have met recently. Of course your friends will continue to love you because they always do, but you may be relying slightly more on newcomers to your life. Make sure this doesn't put anyone's nose out of joint.

13 FRIDAY ☿ *Moon Age Day 9   Moon Sign Libra*

am . . . .

pm . . . .
Today responds best if you remain flexible and take the fallibility of others
in your stride. In the main you can show the kindest and most sensitive
side of your nature now and across the weekend, but your nature
becomes less reactive and a little dulled. For that you can thank the arrival
of a twelfth-house Moon tomorrow.

14 SATURDAY ☿ *Moon Age Day 10   Moon Sign Scorpio*

am . . . .

pm . . . .
Even if this isn't the most dynamic or exciting weekend you have
experienced this year, it can have its advantages. For one thing you could
have a little more time on your hands, which you can spend in more or
less any way that takes your fancy. You can afford to do things today that
you want to do – not that you have to.

15 SUNDAY ☿ *Moon Age Day 11   Moon Sign Scorpio*

am . . . .

pm . . . .
Stretch credibility a little today when dealing with people who are
normally far from surprising. You may have someone quite wrong and if
you encourage them a little they could come up trumps in a way you have
never expected. The Archer knows a lot about life and people, but you
are not always the fountain of wisdom that you think.

	LOVE		MONEY		CAREER		VITALITY	
5 +									+ 5
4 +									+ 4
3 +									+ 3
2 +									+ 2
1 +									+ 1
1 –									– 1
2 –									– 2
3 –									– 3
4 –									– 4
5 –									– 5

16 MONDAY ☿ *Moon Age Day 12* *Moon Sign Scorpio*

am . . . .

pm . . . .
The start of a new working week may not seem particularly inspiring, but as the day advances you could discover that things are getting more exciting – and without any intervention on your part. All you have to do in order to become more involved and connected is to pay attention to what is happening.

17 TUESDAY ☿ *Moon Age Day 13* *Moon Sign Sagittarius*

am . . . .

pm . . . .
The Archer can get right back in gear and be eager to get on with things. You needn't brook any sort of interference and should be just about as pushy and determined as it is possible for you to be. The lunar high is a time of potential success and a period during which you can shock and surprise others with your know-how and dexterity.

18 WEDNESDAY ☿ *Moon Age Day 14* *Moon Sign Sagittarius*

am . . . .

pm . . . .
Don't be afraid to keep up the pressure to have things your own way. This isn't necessarily selfish, particularly if you make certain that others benefit from your efforts as well. You need change and diversity and would certainly gain a great deal from any journey you chose to undertake at the moment.

19 THURSDAY ☿ *Moon Age Day 15* *Moon Sign Capricorn*

am . . . .

pm . . . .
Trends suggest it is more and more important to avoid confrontations, especially with colleagues. You may not be quite as sure of yourself as you should be and in any case you can be plain wrong on occasions. The more you push an issue, the greater is the chance that you will end up having to eat humble pie, which tastes awful!

20 FRIDAY
☿ *Moon Age Day 16   Moon Sign Capricorn*

am . . . .

pm . . . .
It is the practical side of life that is favoured at the moment, and you should have little difficulty getting things done. Your mechanical skills are enhanced and working out how things work could be a piece of cake. Even the most complicated tasks are possible for you now if you break them down into their component parts.

21 SATURDAY
Moon Age Day 17   Moon Sign Capricorn

am . . . .

pm . . . .
The analytical side of your nature continues to be emphasised, and this works for you far beyond the world of the practical. Working out how other people are likely to behave under any given circumstance can give you a distinct edge, and you could shock one or two people if your predictions turn out to be correct.

22 SUNDAY
Moon Age Day 18   Moon Sign Aquarius

am . . . .

pm . . . .
An ideal time to get together with friends and agree a way forward that brings new input and more interesting happenings into your life. Friendship is extremely important at the moment and is especially significant when you are dealing with people you have known for years. If there has been a rift, you can now heal the breach quite easily.

	LOVE	MONEY	CAREER	VITALITY
5 +				+ 5
4 +				+ 4
3 +				+ 3
2 +				+ 2
1 +				+ 1
1 -				- 1
2 -				- 2
3 -				- 3
4 -				- 4
5 -				- 5

23 MONDAY   *Moon Age Day 19   Moon Sign Aquarius*

am . . . .

pm . . . .
Trends assist you to know what you want right now and to have ideas about how you can get it. The only problem seems to be that other people may not agree and that can lead to some sort of confrontation. This is not necessary if you manage yourself well and if you continue to turn up your intuition. The important people should still love you today.

24 TUESDAY   *Moon Age Day 20   Moon Sign Pisces*

am . . . .

pm . . . .
There are signs that arrangements may have to be changed, perhaps at the last moment. As long as you check and double-check all details everything should work out fine. Not everyone may be on your side, though you might be slightly too suspicious for your own good at some stage today.

25 WEDNESDAY   *Moon Age Day 21   Moon Sign Pisces*

am . . . .

pm . . . .
Your strength lies in showing regard for the feelings and general sensibilities of those around you and finding time to spend with family members. At the same time the romantic possibilities are better, offering you scope to think up better and more convincing words of love for your partner.

26 THURSDAY   *Moon Age Day 22   Moon Sign Pisces*

am . . . .

pm . . . .
As the month draws on so it may occur to you that there are things to be done that you haven't begun to address yet. The fact is that even the Archer can only do so much, and even if you work hard from morning until night your expectations of yourself are often too great. Why not just be thankful for what you have already achieved?

27 FRIDAY
Moon Age Day 23   Moon Sign Aries

am . . . .

pm . . . .
They say that slow and steady wins the race, though this is an adage that
might as well be Chinese as far as you are concerned. Maybe you should
learn what it means though, because constantly rushing today won't get
you anywhere. Better by far now to do one job well than to mess up a
dozen and have to do them all over again.

28 SATURDAY
Moon Age Day 24   Moon Sign Aries

am . . . .

pm . . . .
Keep looking and concentrating – that's the way to get ahead at present.
If not everyone is equally helpful to you at the moment, it could be that
they are simply chasing their own rainbows and are unaware of yours.
Dreams can be shared and all it takes is a conversation or two that will
lead to better co-operation and common goals.

29 SUNDAY
Moon Age Day 25   Moon Sign Taurus

am . . . .

pm . . . .
The more you alter situations today, the better things are likely to turn
out. If there is one thing the Archer hates it is convention. A little upset
of the applecart is required in order for you to bring some more interest
into your life. Of course not everyone is going to approve, but if you
always waited for approval you'd never get anything done!

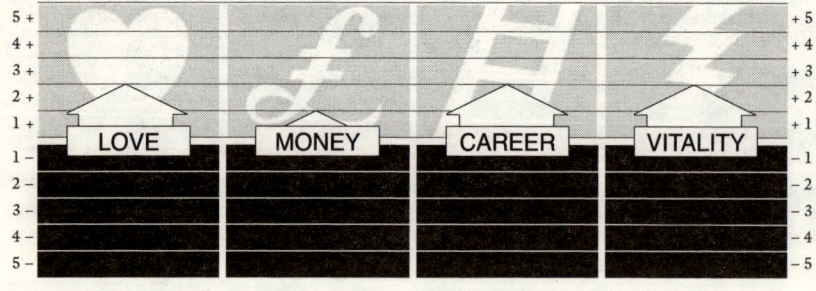

30 MONDAY
Moon Age Day 26   Moon Sign Taurus

am . . . .

pm . . . .
This is going to be a week of mixed fortunes but it can be helped no end if you get a positive start. If there is something you want to do today, get on with it quickly because it will become increasingly difficult to follow your own initiatives. Be prepared to enlist the support of colleagues or friends, and go for gold without any thought of failure.

1 TUESDAY
Moon Age Day 27   Moon Sign Gemini

am . . . .

pm . . . .
The start of a new month could bring its own slight problems, thanks to the arrival of the lunar low. Whilst the Moon occupies the zodiac sign of Gemini you are encouraged into quiet corners or shunted into sidings that you know can lead you nowhere. Fighting back is not your ideal response. Patience is what is needed.

2 WEDNESDAY
Moon Age Day 28   Moon Sign Gemini

am . . . .

pm . . . .
You would be wise to guard against any sense of impending doom, which may simply be a response to a more pessimistic interlude. By tomorrow, you can get everything back to normal but for the moment you could feel as though all your efforts are in vain. You have a good flair for the dramatic!

3 THURSDAY
Moon Age Day 0   Moon Sign Cancer

am . . . .

pm . . . .
Any concern you managed to create for yourself yesterday can be dissipated almost as soon as you get out of bed today. The fact is that you can now get more or less back to normal, but your anxiety could well have affected those close to you. That's typical of the Archer and maybe an apology is in order?

99

4 FRIDAY

Moon Age Day 1   Moon Sign Cancer

am . . . .

pm . . . .
As the weekend approaches you can afford to become ever more confident about your ideas and opinions. Whether or not the world at large is as sure of your point of view as you are remains to be seen, but you do have good powers of persuasion. It's worth using these to convince others that you know what you are talking about.

5 SATURDAY

Moon Age Day 2   Moon Sign Leo

am . . . .

pm . . . .
The likelihood that you are becoming restless is strong, and that means you may have to change certain things if you are not to become bored with your life. Any form of travel would suit you down to the ground and it looks as though you can get a great deal from all locations that have a strong artistic or historical heritage.

6 SUNDAY

Moon Age Day 3   Moon Sign Leo

am . . . .

pm . . . .
An ideal day to get together with others, especially for purely social reasons, and enjoy the cut and thrust of simple conversation. You are sometimes so busy that you fail to realise that communication is one of the most important components of your nature. It doesn't matter what is being said today because you can have an interest in everything.

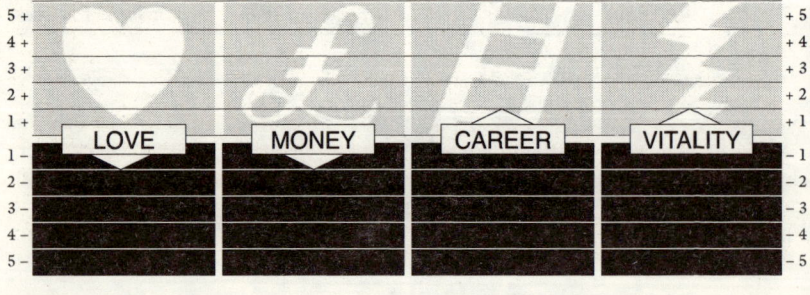

July 2008

YOUR MONTH AT A GLANCE

⊕ = Opportunities are around   ⊖ = Be on the defensive   ⬤ = Life is pretty ordinary

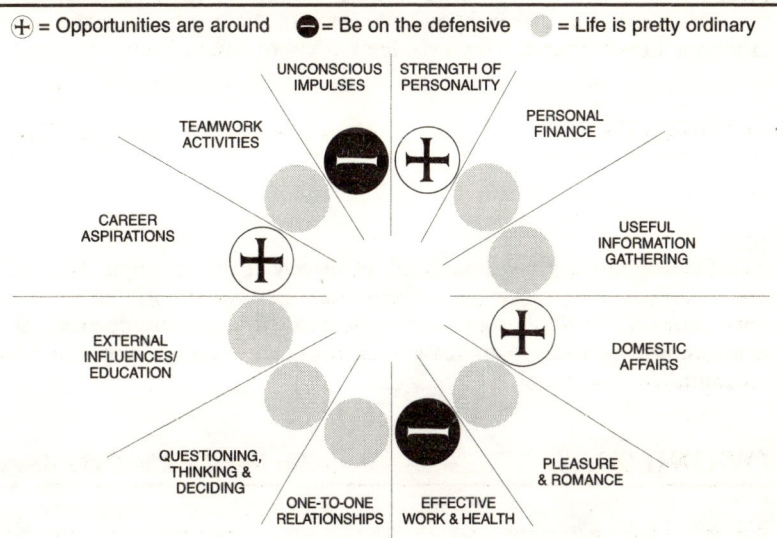

UNCONSCIOUS IMPULSES
STRENGTH OF PERSONALITY
TEAMWORK ACTIVITIES
PERSONAL FINANCE
CAREER ASPIRATIONS
USEFUL INFORMATION GATHERING
EXTERNAL INFLUENCES/ EDUCATION
DOMESTIC AFFAIRS
QUESTIONING, THINKING & DECIDING
PLEASURE & ROMANCE
ONE-TO-ONE RELATIONSHIPS
EFFECTIVE WORK & HEALTH

JULY HIGHS AND LOWS

Here I show you how the rhythms of the Moon will affect you this month. Like the tide, your energies and abilities will rise and fall with its pattern. When it is above the centre line, go for it, when it is below, you should be resting.

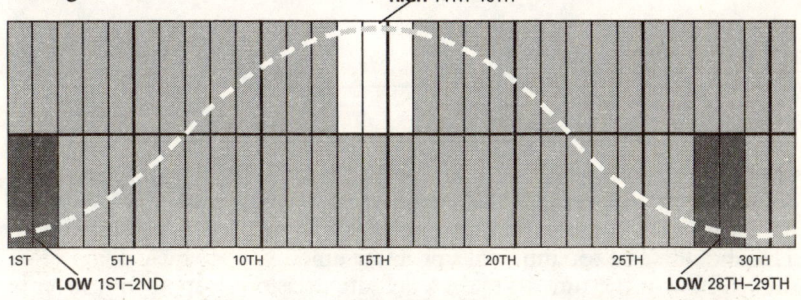

HIGH 14TH–16TH

1ST   5TH   10TH   15TH   20TH   25TH   30TH

LOW 1ST–2ND

LOW 28TH–29TH

7 MONDAY
Moon Age Day 4   Moon Sign Virgo

am . . . .

pm . . . .
This is no time to be rushing your fences. Do it right and you will reap the rewards but if you insist on pushing too hard or in the wrong direction, difficulties could follow. Your fertile mind has potential to work overtime at present and you have some of the most wonderful ideas of the year in your head. Why not defer a few of them?

8 TUESDAY
Moon Age Day 5   Moon Sign Virgo

am . . . .

pm . . . .
You have scope to apply yourself very positively at the moment, even if it seems as if just about everyone else is talking about work rather than getting on with it. Never mind, if you want anything doing properly, it's worth doing it yourself in any case. Routines can be something of a bind at present.

9 WEDNESDAY
Moon Age Day 6   Moon Sign Libra

am . . . .

pm . . . .
You can now set the seal on some important plans, though you might have to change your mind at the last minute in some instances. Nothing is set in stone for you just at the moment but at least you can be flexible enough not to worry too much about that. Your creative potential is getting better and better around this time.

10 THURSDAY
Moon Age Day 7   Moon Sign Libra

am . . . .

pm . . . .
Standard responses in personal attachments may not work and you might have to put in some extra effort to please your partner or sweetheart. This shouldn't be too much of a problem unless you are busy doing other things. Now is the time to make a definite decision to spoil your lover in some way.

11 FRIDAY
Moon Age Day 8   Moon Sign Libra

am . . . .

pm . . . .
If colleagues or friends seem indecisive it may be necessary for you to make most of the decisions. That is hardly a trial for the Archer but it could be slightly awkward taking everyone into account. All in all it might seem as if life would be much simpler at the moment if you only had yourself to please. It's important to keep smiling.

12 SATURDAY
Moon Age Day 9   Moon Sign Scorpio

am . . . .

pm . . . .
Even if intimate relationships still prove to be somewhat demanding, you can make sure they are sizzling all the same. Sagittarius is at its sensual best and it isn't hard for you to make people take notice of you. The fact that you attract compliments is no coincidence and is down to your magnetism.

13 SUNDAY
Moon Age Day 10   Moon Sign Scorpio

am . . . .

pm . . . .
You may not always get the reactions you expect from others today, which completes a week or so during which you have had to look very closely at those around you in order to make certain you are pleasing them. By tomorrow the emphasis will have changed but for today you may decide to spend time with family members.

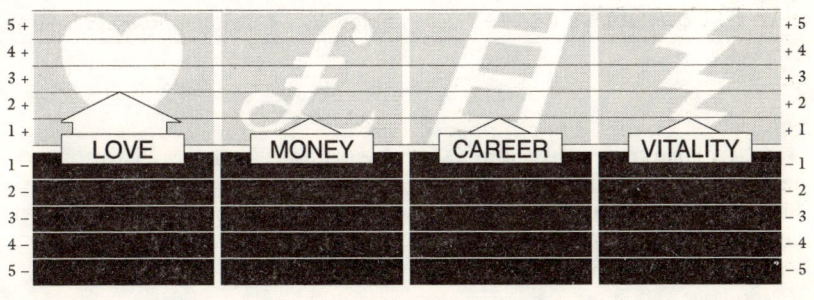

14 MONDAY
Moon Age Day 11   Moon Sign Sagittarius

am . . . .

pm . . . .

The new working week starts on a good note as the lunar high brings newer and better opportunities into your life. You can capitalise on the luck that is on your side, but much of your success today is down to being in the right place at the most opportune time. Your ability to deal with others is enhanced this week.

15 TUESDAY
Moon Age Day 12   Moon Sign Sagittarius

am . . . .

pm . . . .

There are a number of gains to be made today and most of them come as a result of your very dynamic approach to life in a general sense. You can show yourself to be ingenious whilst at the same time maintaining a cheerful and attractive attitude. This is the time of the month to catapult yourself into new and fascinating relationships.

16 WEDNESDAY
Moon Age Day 13   Moon Sign Sagittarius

am . . . .

pm . . . .

Lady Luck should still be on your side and you ought to be willing to push things a little whilst trends are so good. If there is something about which you have been in a puzzle you can now rely on your strong intuition to find the answers you need. You can also get yourself in the good books of people who are also filled with good ideas.

17 THURSDAY
Moon Age Day 14   Moon Sign Capricorn

am . . . .

pm . . . .

This is a very favourable time to involve yourself in new social ventures, and a period to wander about more. As the summer really opens up, the lure of travel becomes ever more obvious. If there is one thing the Archer hates it is to be stuck in the same place for days or weeks on end, so it's especially beneficial to plan a journey now.

18 FRIDAY *Moon Age Day 15* *Moon Sign Capricorn*

am . . . .

pm . . . .
There are positive social highlights on the horizon, probably for the forthcoming weekend. However, if nothing specific is in the pipeline it will be up to you to do something about it. There's no point in waiting for others to make a move, and in any case you can persuade most of those close to you to follow your lead.

19 SATURDAY *Moon Age Day 16* *Moon Sign Aquarius*

am . . . .

pm . . . .
You can display a very warm-hearted attitude across the weekend and should be noticed by almost everyone. It's easy for you to smile at the moment if things are going your way. At the same time you know instinctively how to please others and might be particularly affectionate towards your partner and close family members.

20 SUNDAY *Moon Age Day 17* *Moon Sign Aquarius*

am . . . .

pm . . . .
Personal encounters continue to be important and to offer you the very best of what life has in store for you. Don't be too quick to follow the lead of other people. You have what it takes to steer people in the right direction – with a mixture of simply psychology and gentle force.

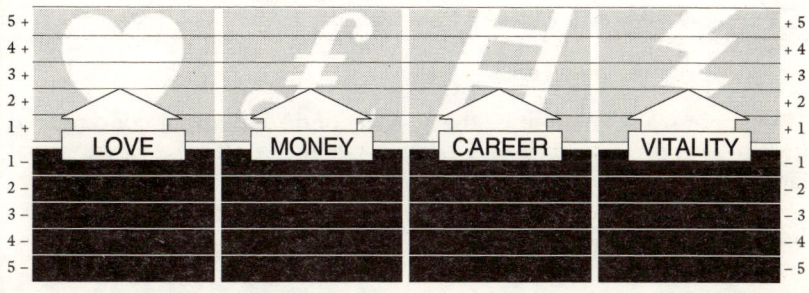

21 MONDAY
Moon Age Day 18   Moon Sign Aquarius

am . . . .

pm . . . .
Life remains potentially harmonious, but also busy and fairly demanding.
You have the ability to deal with pressure very well at the moment and
needn't feel stressed. The same may not be the case for friends, so be
prepared to support them throughout much of this week.

22 TUESDAY
Moon Age Day 19   Moon Sign Pisces

am . . . .

pm . . . .
Romance is well starred, though opportunities could come when you
least expect them. The Archer is very attractive to others but can also be
quite naïve on occasions. As a result you could find that you have
admirers you never even suspected. Keep a sense of proportion when it
comes to finances, at least until Friday or Saturday.

23 WEDNESDAY
Moon Age Day 20   Moon Sign Pisces

am . . . .

pm . . . .
This is not a good day to get behind yourself, which is why it would be
sensible to rise very early and to pitch into jobs as quickly and efficiently
as you can. Later on you can afford to please yourself, though this could
be difficult if you haven't achieved all you wanted. All the same, you can't
be in two places at the same time.

24 THURSDAY
Moon Age Day 21   Moon Sign Aries

am . . . .

pm . . . .
This is not really going to be the best day of the month for concentrated
work that requires precision or logic. On the contrary, a more casual
approach is encouraged whilst the Moon occupies its present position in
your solar chart. If you know this to be the case it might be best to leave
some things until later.

25 FRIDAY
Moon Age Day 22   Moon Sign Aries

am . . . .

pm . . . .
You may still be dealing more in possibilities than certainties, though your hunches are generally very good and you can at least afford to explore a few potentials. Don't get too tied down with any one task, especially if it is something you always see as being tedious. Why not leave it until another day, whilst you have fun?

26 SATURDAY
Moon Age Day 23   Moon Sign Taurus

am . . . .

pm . . . .
Relationships continue to bring out the best in you, as they have been doing throughout much of July. You are presently in a position to make the best of impressions on people who could do you a lot of good in the future, though your attitude is far from being mercenary. The Archer can be at its most pleasant.

27 SUNDAY
Moon Age Day 24   Moon Sign Taurus

am . . . .

pm . . . .
Focus on material priorities today, particularly if you have been ignoring them of late. That doesn't mean you should sit and pore over the family accounts all day and you can certainly afford to split your time so that at least some hours are spent doing enjoyable things. Sporting activities could offer you scope for success.

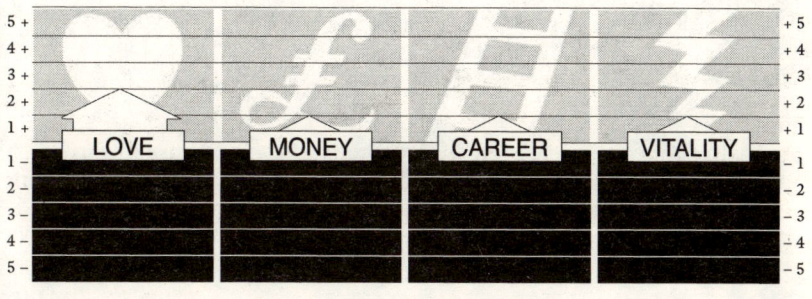

28 MONDAY
Moon Age Day 25   Moon Sign Gemini

am . . . .

pm . . . .
As the Moon moves into Gemini, so you may have slightly less energy available than before, and might be fairly happy to sit still from time to time. As a rule this doesn't please you at all because it is the essence of your nature to be always on the go. An ideal day for a comfortable chair and a really good book.

29 TUESDAY
Moon Age Day 26   Moon Sign Gemini

am . . . .

pm . . . .
You might not be quite as precise as necessary at the moment because the lunar low this time around encourages a more vague approach. All the same, its power to have any great bearing on your life is limited and you can afford to coast through the Moon's residence in Gemini if you can get others to take the strain.

30 WEDNESDAY
Moon Age Day 27   Moon Sign Cancer

am . . . .

pm . . . .
Today offers you scope to build walls, though these are designed to support relationships rather than to block them out. The more you do for others at the moment the greater will be their regard for you. The Archer is going through its most selfless stage for months, and all because it feels so good to be kind to everyone.

31 THURSDAY
Moon Age Day 28   Moon Sign Cancer

am . . . .

pm . . . .
All matters of communication are favoured, and you can use this trend to get on side with people you haven't instinctively liked all that much in the past. Yours is probably the most flexible of all the zodiac signs and it is possible for you to be a very different person on any two consecutive days.

1 FRIDAY

Moon Age Day 0   Moon Sign Leo

am . . . .

pm . . . .
With the first day of August comes a strong desire to spread your wings.
The slightly more introspective spell that has perpetuated during July is
now starting to give way to greater energy and more personal
determination. Nevertheless, if you have made valuable allies across the
last few weeks they should continue to help you out.

2 SATURDAY

Moon Age Day 1   Moon Sign Leo

am . . . .

pm . . . .
Any obligations that you feel today may prevent you from doing exactly
what you would wish, though you can still find enjoyment in routines.
Money matters can be strengthened, perhaps as a result of your actions
in the past. Follow up on new and revolutionary ideas that come into
your head around now.

3 SUNDAY

Moon Age Day 2   Moon Sign Virgo

am . . . .

pm . . . .
Even if you remain generally positive and aspiring, the deeper side of your
nature is also in operation. It isn't so much what people do that fascinates
you right now but rather the motives that underpin their actions. The
world is filled with fascination and wonder – which is part of what makes
being a Sagittarian so amazing.

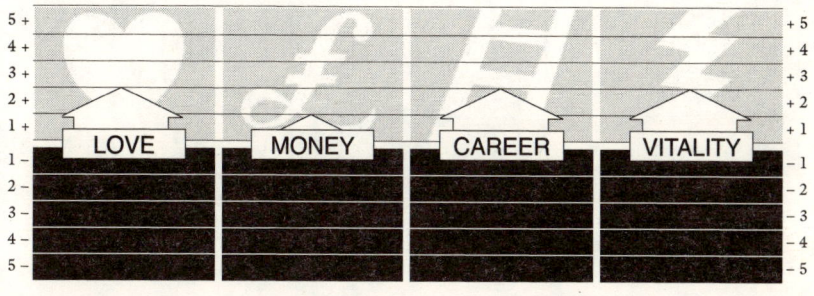

August 2008

YOUR MONTH AT A GLANCE

⊕ = Opportunities are around ⊖ = Be on the defensive ● = Life is pretty ordinary

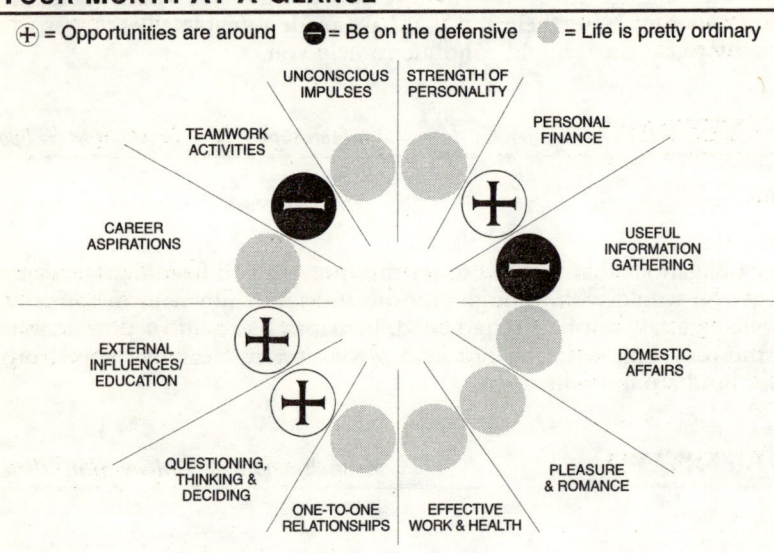

UNCONSCIOUS IMPULSES

STRENGTH OF PERSONALITY

TEAMWORK ACTIVITIES

PERSONAL FINANCE

CAREER ASPIRATIONS

USEFUL INFORMATION GATHERING

EXTERNAL INFLUENCES/ EDUCATION

DOMESTIC AFFAIRS

QUESTIONING, THINKING & DECIDING

ONE-TO-ONE RELATIONSHIPS

EFFECTIVE WORK & HEALTH

PLEASURE & ROMANCE

AUGUST HIGHS AND LOWS

Here I show you how the rhythms of the Moon will affect you this month. Like the tide, your energies and abilities will rise and fall with its pattern. When it is above the centre line, go for it, when it is below, you should be resting.

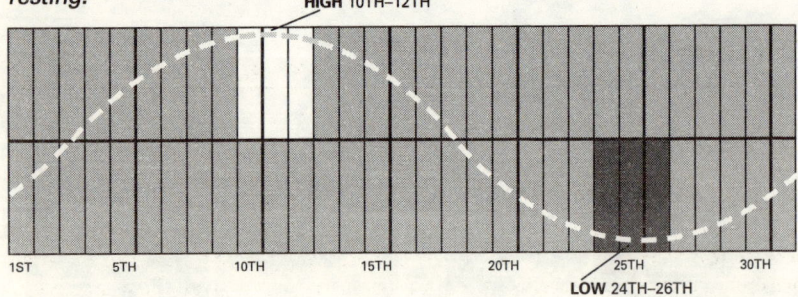

HIGH 10TH–12TH

1ST   5TH   10TH   15TH   20TH   25TH   30TH

LOW 24TH–26TH

4 MONDAY
Moon Age Day 3   Moon Sign Virgo

am . . . .

pm . . . .
Your competitive attitude when in social settings could stimulate some tension between yourself and others. You may also need to give those around you the benefit of the doubt just at the moment, even if you suspect in your heart or hearts that they are working against your own best interests.

5 TUESDAY
Moon Age Day 4   Moon Sign Virgo

am . . . .

pm . . . .
This can be a first-class time from a professional point of view, particularly if you show everyone just how capable you can be. Recent efforts could be paying off well and you can persuade others to take notice of what you have to say. The same may not be entirely true at home, where getting attention may be tricky.

6 WEDNESDAY
Moon Age Day 5   Moon Sign Libra

am . . . .

pm . . . .
Your general daily routines could be affected by small mishaps, leading you to a situation that means repeating yourself. You would be wise not to overrate the possibility of a lucky break coming along at just the right time, because in the main you will only get out what you put in around now. There is luck – but you manufacture it yourself.

7 THURSDAY
Moon Age Day 6   Moon Sign Libra

am . . . .

pm . . . .
Work and practical matters have potential to keep you fairly busy, and there may not be much time for social situations or other diversions. In reality you may not want too much outside of your practical life because present astrological trends do little to boost your available energy. A comfortable chair in the sun might appeal around now.

8 FRIDAY
Moon Age Day 7   Moon Sign Scorpio

am . . . .

pm . . . .
This can be a fairly progressive period but one that is more likely to be dedicated to planning rather than doing. Getting yourself organised should prove to be easy, even if others are looking on rather than helping you out. Stay your hand for the moment because the real action comes in a day or two. Family ties are emphasised now.

9 SATURDAY
Moon Age Day 8   Moon Sign Scorpio

am . . . .

pm . . . .
Friends and family, and your commitment to them, are to the fore. With the Moon in your solar twelfth house you show a desire for peace and quiet, though whether you can get as much of that commodity as you would wish remains to be seen.

10 SUNDAY
Moon Age Day 9   Moon Sign Sagittarius

am . . . .

pm . . . .
Along comes an excellent time to put your luck to the test. The lunar high for August is likely to be very potent, and whilst it might not bring you your heart's desire, it can help you to go a long way in that direction. All that is required in some cases is the finishing touch, and you have what it takes to put full stops to situations quite easily today.

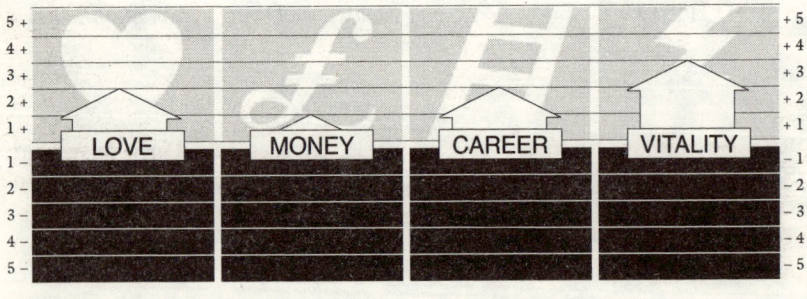

11 MONDAY   *Moon Age Day 10   Moon Sign Sagittarius*

am ....

pm ....
You can continue to get life going your way, which at the moment tends
to be the way you choose. You can certainly benefit from putting new
ideas to the test and have scope to take other people along with you on
whatever adventure takes your present fancy. This would be a good time
of the month to take a holiday.

12 TUESDAY   *Moon Age Day 11   Moon Sign Sagittarius*

am ....

pm ....
For the third day in a row you can be positive in your attitude and
capable in your actions. What really matters at the moment is the positive
impression you are able to make on others. If you want to influence your
boss or more experienced colleagues, now is the time to unleash plans
and ideas that have been floating around in your head.

13 WEDNESDAY   *Moon Age Day 12   Moon Sign Capricorn*

am ....

pm ....
Change and movement is important for the Archer at the best of times,
but is fairly crucial at the moment. There are gains to be made from
following unusual ideas and from pursuing something that others see as
being a lost cause. The fact is that you simply won't be beaten right now,
and that gets you noticed all the more.

14 THURSDAY   *Moon Age Day 13   Moon Sign Capricorn*

am ....

pm ....
Be ready for and open to all new experiences, even those that take you
completely by surprise. It takes a lot to shake your equilibrium but the
casual remarks of others today could do the trick. Perhaps you are about
to discover that you have admirers you never suspected? Play it cool and
don't show any embarrassment.

15 FRIDAY

Moon Age Day 14   Moon Sign Aquarius

am . . . .

pm . . . .
You may not be entirely satisfied with anything today – that is unless you
get the chance to sort things out for yourself. If you don't trust others at
the moment you may be very picky when you are following in the
footsteps of another. Even the Archer must learn to trust and to take
some things at face value. Remain adventurous today.

16 SATURDAY

Moon Age Day 15   Moon Sign Aquarius

am . . . .

pm . . . .
Trends suggest that you may need to drop what you are doing to deal
with minor problems at home. In all probability that won't be too much
of a bind on a Saturday, though you have to remember that there are
social possibilities you won't want to miss. Organisation is the key.

17 SUNDAY

Moon Age Day 16   Moon Sign Aquarius

am . . . .

pm . . . .
Love life and romantic issues can be highly rewarding just now and you
have scope to make today one of the happiest and most contented days
of the month so far. If the weather is good you need to be spending time
relaxing – though even this can be a very dynamic and strenuous
experience for the Archer. Spoil your lover today.

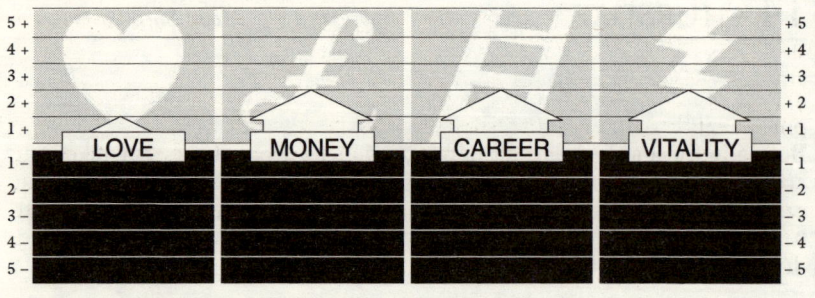

18 MONDAY   *Moon Age Day 17   Moon Sign Pisces*

am . . . .

pm . . . .
The present position of Mercury in your solar chart can offer a definite boost to friendship matters and to all your associations with others. It may also encourage contact with people you haven't had much to do with before, and should heighten the sense of anticipation that is present whenever you embark on something new.

19 TUESDAY   *Moon Age Day 18   Moon Sign Pisces*

am . . . .

pm . . . .
Now you should be at your very best when dealing with practical matters and when things are left to you to be sorted out once and for all. The world really does trust you at present and you needn't let anyone down because you can be so committed to the task at hand. This can also bring a little too much intensity.

20 WEDNESDAY   *Moon Age Day 19   Moon Sign Aries*

am . . . .

pm . . . .
Pointless conflict with others is now a possibility, particularly if you are quite stubborn in your attitude and far less willing to bend with the wind than was the case only a day or two ago. If you try to cultivate your usual flexibility you will get on far better and achieve objectives.

21 THURSDAY   *Moon Age Day 20   Moon Sign Aries*

am . . . .

pm . . . .
Today can be slightly more satisfying, but might still have its problems if you refuse to show a more easy-going attitude to life generally. Little things that others do could so easily annoy you and may cause you to be somewhat grumpy on occasions. It's worth showing a positive response to people you know in your heart are only trying to help.

22 FRIDAY
Moon Age Day 21   Moon Sign Taurus

am . . . .

pm . . . .
Even if your social life is less inspiring today, you can ensure it recovers before the weekend arrives. Maybe others let you down over an arrangement, or circumstances prevent you from following an already organised plan. Once again you need to show patience and show how resilient you are capable of being.

23 SATURDAY
Moon Age Day 22   Moon Sign Taurus

am . . . .

pm . . . .
Today can act as a breath of fresh air after a few days during which trends haven't helped you to give of your best. Just when it really counts you come good and can enjoy yourself tremendously, no matter what you decide to do. The choice tends to be yours today and you needn't be hidebound by routine or expectation.

24 SUNDAY
Moon Age Day 23   Moon Sign Gemini

am . . . .

pm . . . .
It's possible that energy will be in short supply today and that you won't feel like pushing yourself too hard. With the lunar low around you may decide to settle for a seat in the sun or for cruising around in the car to some place you love. Don't have too many practical expectations at the moment and you can't go far wrong.

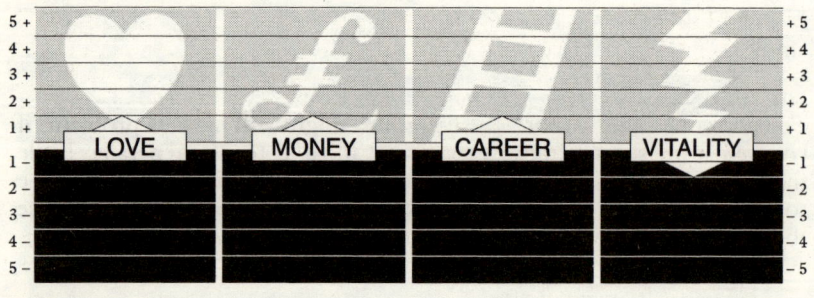

25 MONDAY

Moon Age Day 24   *Moon Sign Gemini*

am . . . .

pm . . . .
Although this may not be the most positive start to a new week that you
are ever likely to experience, you can still make some progress in a general
sense. Just don't expect too much and avoid taking on more than you
know you can handle. This is a time to recharge your batteries and not a
period for burning yourself out.

26 TUESDAY

Moon Age Day 25   *Moon Sign Gemini*

am . . . .

pm . . . .
From a potentially slow start today you should be able to get things on
the move again by the middle of the afternoon. The time is right for a
complete change of scenery and if this particular wish cannot be gratified
at work you may have to ring the changes once you finish and create an
evening to remember.

27 WEDNESDAY

Moon Age Day 26   *Moon Sign Cancer*

am . . . .

pm . . . .
Prevailing influences suggest mistrust and vulnerability regarding a
personal matter. Although you want to trust other people, their actions
could make this quite difficult. It is possible that you have got hold of the
wrong end of the stick and a complete reappraisal of situations may be in
order at some stage today.

28 THURSDAY

Moon Age Day 27   *Moon Sign Cancer*

am . . . .

pm . . . .
You have what it takes to make steady progress towards career goals – but
when was 'steady' progress ever enough for the Archer? All the same, you
could find that things begin to go wrong if you really put on the pressure,
and would be well advised to pace yourself in almost anything you do. A
day to look for new social interests.

29 FRIDAY
Moon Age Day 28   Moon Sign Leo

am . . . .

pm . . . .
Certain friendships have a lot going for them at the moment and can help you to create personal freedom and space. Even if not everyone seems to be on your side at this time, you can still seek help from people you have known the longest. Do your best to give them as much as they are offering you.

30 SATURDAY
Moon Age Day 29   Moon Sign Leo

am . . . .

pm . . . .
A slightly difficult aspect of Mercury now supports a period of some slight mental confusion. It isn't necessarily that you are getting anything totally wrong, merely that you might fall down when it comes to those important little details that can make all the difference. You may decide to rely on others at some stage today.

31 SUNDAY
Moon Age Day 0   Moon Sign Virgo

am . . . .

pm . . . .
If it seems that your love life and romantic matters generally are in the doldrums, your best response is to put in some extra effort. Even then you may not be at your happiest with those around you. Friends may well offer more satisfaction than your lover or family members, but this is a very temporary state of affairs.

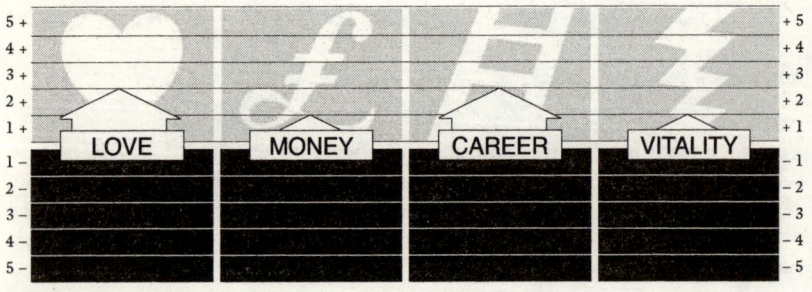

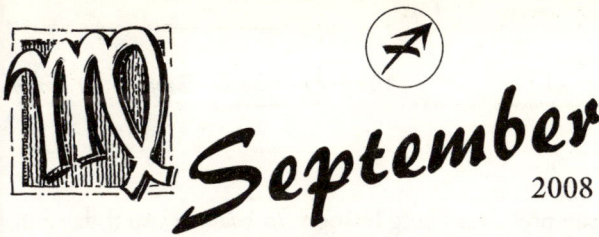

September

2008

YOUR MONTH AT A GLANCE

$\oplus$ = Opportunities are around $\ominus$ = Be on the defensive   ● = Life is pretty ordinary

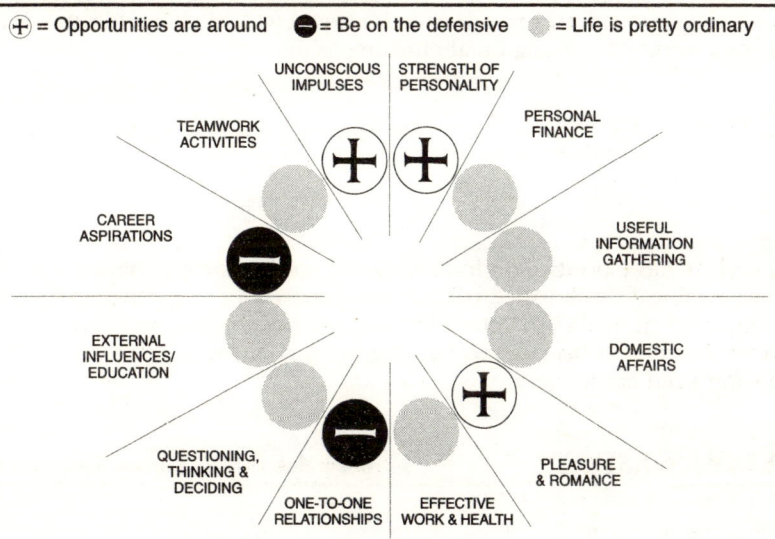

SEPTEMBER HIGHS AND LOWS

Here I show you how the rhythms of the Moon will affect you this month. Like the tide, your energies and abilities will rise and fall with its pattern. When it is above the centre line, go for it, when it is below, you should be resting.

HIGH 7TH–8TH

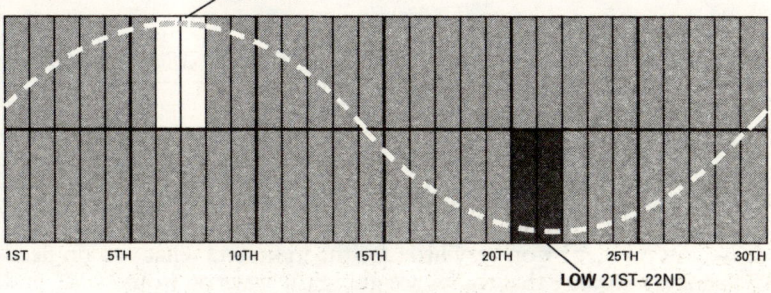

LOW 21ST–22ND

119

1 MONDAY

Moon Age Day 1   Moon Sign Virgo

am . . . .

pm . . . .
There could be certain pressures being brought to bear on you today and
most of these are likely to come from home. Professional matters have
potential to be more successful than personal ambitions and it is therefore
towards your work that trends encourage you to turn. It could seem as if
almost everyone is going on about something.

2 TUESDAY

Moon Age Day 2   Moon Sign Libra

am . . . .

pm . . . .
A slightly more positive outlook is possible today and you have scope to
master a few difficult issues, particularly if you adopt a very matter-of-fact
attitude to them. When others see you are not worried or preoccupied
they too will tend to fall into line. By the end of the day you should be
leading from the front.

3 WEDNESDAY

Moon Age Day 3   Moon Sign Libra

am . . . .

pm . . . .
The planets offer you one of the best days of the month for being with
others and for getting on well with life generally. You can afford to seek
out good company and to surround yourself with luxury if that proves to
be possible. Responsibilities needn't bother you too much under present
trends.

4 THURSDAY

Moon Age Day 4   Moon Sign Scorpio

am . . . .

pm . . . .
Stand by for a few days that could well be quieter and which might offer
you less in material terms. In a way that shouldn't bother you at all
because you can get by on very little for the moment. What you do need
is constant reassurance that things are going the way you would wish, and
that might mean badgering people a little.

5 FRIDAY
Moon Age Day 5   Moon Sign Scorpio

am . . . .

pm . . . .
You might still be slightly lacking in conviction, and respond best when everyone tells you how right you are. Although to the world at large the Archer might seem to be the most self-assured and confident person in the world, this is not always the case. But at least you can give a good impression and sometimes that is enough.

6 SATURDAY
Moon Age Day 6   Moon Sign Scorpio

am . . . .

pm . . . .
Your powers of concentration are not enhanced, so beware of doing too much or taking on issues that are not really your responsibility at all. Better by far today to do what is expected of you and then to get on with something that simply pleases you. There are ways to delight your lover and you know what they are.

7 SUNDAY
Moon Age Day 7   Moon Sign Sagittarius

am . . . .

pm . . . .
There are gains to be made if you make an early start today and get on with doing something that really pleases you, as well as being of practical benefit. There is really no limit to your capabilities at this time, a situation enhanced by the lunar high. The Archer can also be very competitive today.

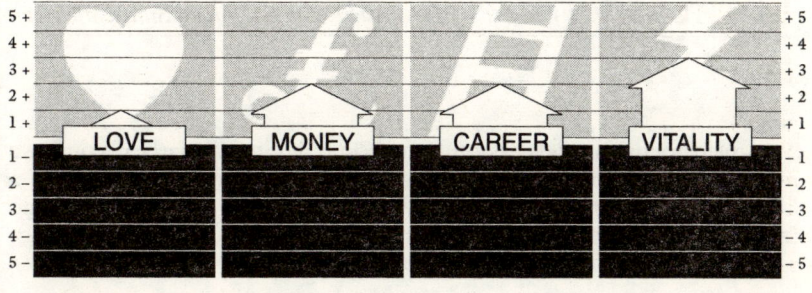

8 MONDAY   *Moon Age Day 8   Moon Sign Sagittarius*

am . . . .

pm . . . .
There could come a reminder today that things are far better than you
might have expected. The fact is that the lunar high offers you all the
support you could possibly need and can help you to get into the most
positive frame of mind that you will experience in the whole month of
September. Use these advantages.

9 TUESDAY   *Moon Age Day 9   Moon Sign Capricorn*

am . . . .

pm . . . .
If there is a fly in the ointment today it could be that family relationships
are not quite as strong as you might wish them to be. Even if this state
of affairs is not your fault, you can do something towards sorting it out.
Don't get too tied down with details today because a broad overview will
work best for you.

10 WEDNESDAY   *Moon Age Day 10   Moon Sign Capricorn*

am . . . .

pm . . . .
It might seem as though you have to work extra hard today in order to
get to your objectives, but the effort can be more than worthwhile. You
are having some very good ideas and it only takes a little more effort to
turn some of these into concrete realities. Why not enlist the support of
colleagues at work and friends closer to home?

11 THURSDAY   *Moon Age Day 11   Moon Sign Capricorn*

am . . . .

pm . . . .
The main focus for today is on your home life, particularly if you have
more time on your hands than you expected. Archers who have been a
little off-colour of late should be taking things fairly steadily but an
improvement is possible. Don't be too quick to pick up the traces of
responsibilities that are not really yours.

12 FRIDAY   *Moon Age Day 12   Moon Sign Aquarius*

am . . . .

pm . . . .
You can now gain the trust and confidence of those around you and in particular people you work with. It's good to know that you have their confidence but you may also be enjoying or enduring extra work as a result. This might be because you are such a willing horse, and the best way out of it is to delegate.

13 SATURDAY   *Moon Age Day 13   Moon Sign Aquarius*

am . . . .

pm . . . .
The present position of Mars in your solar chart offers more challenging times, but ones you tend to relish. You now prefer spontaneity instead of planning, and have what it takes to sort things out on the move. New relationships can be formed at this time, and it's worth being quite definite in terms of what you are seeking.

14 SUNDAY   *Moon Age Day 14   Moon Sign Pisces*

am . . . .

pm . . . .
This is not an ideal time for logical planning, and your best approach may be to make up your mind on the spur of the moment. Your strength lies in gathering others around you and eliciting compliments, always a good psychological spur to a Sagittarian.

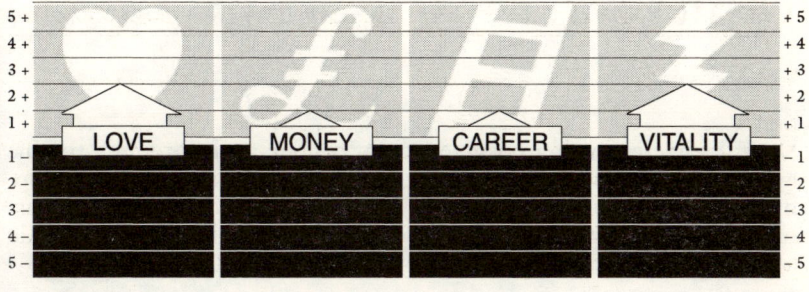

15 MONDAY
Moon Age Day 15   Moon Sign Pisces

am . . . .

pm . . . .
Creative endeavours are particularly well accented today, offering you a chance to try new incentives and ideas. Not everyone may be equally positive, and there could be some fairly awkward types to deal with on the way. If you refuse to let this shake your own equilibrium you can really get on well today.

16 TUESDAY
Moon Age Day 16   Moon Sign Aries

am . . . .

pm . . . .
It's time to get down to business and to deal with any issues that have been put on the back burner for a while. Your organisational skills are now enhanced, and it shouldn't be difficult to get colleagues, friends or family members to accept their own responsibilities. The Archer is definitely in charge!

17 WEDNESDAY
Moon Age Day 17   Moon Sign Aries

am . . . .

pm . . . .
Social meetings and talks about almost anything are now favoured, and the Archer could be at its most chatty at this stage of the month. You enjoy being in good company and have what it takes to be both entertaining and funny. There's no wonder everyone wants to have you on board. Professional matters are also well starred.

18 THURSDAY
Moon Age Day 18   Moon Sign Aries

am . . . .

pm . . . .
Stand by to deal with a possible lack of confidence regarding a specific matter. This needn't last long and in reality might be a storm in a teacup, but it might have a bearing on your decision-making during the first part of the day. Be prepared to respond very positively to the cheerful attitude of family members at this time.

19 FRIDAY   *Moon Age Day 19   Moon Sign Taurus*

am . . . .

pm . . . .
Happiness for you is being on the move. There's nothing strange about this because the Archer hates to be tied down to the same spot for very long. Now is the time to travel whenever the opportunity presents itself, and to do all you can to see new sights and to experience aspects of life that are strange to you.

20 SATURDAY   *Moon Age Day 20   Moon Sign Taurus*

am . . . .

pm . . . .
If something from your past now crops up again, you may decide to deal with it in a very different way than you did previously. You can be quite thoughtful, especially later on today, and you may choose to retreat more and more into your own shell. For this you can thank the arriving lunar low.

21 SUNDAY   *Moon Age Day 21   Moon Sign Gemini*

am . . . .

pm . . . .
A potential lull is now in operation and you won't help your cause by trying harder than is strictly necessary to do anything. On the contrary you would be far better off watching and waiting, whilst you allow other people to do most of the work. You can afford to trust in their abilities to get things right and to work on your behalf.

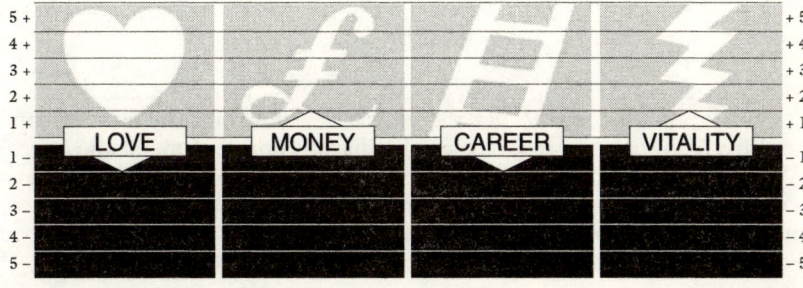

22 MONDAY   *Moon Age Day 22   Moon Sign Gemini*

am . . . .

pm . . . .
Beware of being too impulsive for your own good just now. It's worth
checking things out fully before commiting yourself. Better by far to
delay most important decisions when it proves to be possible or to let
someone you trust decide on something that puzzles you.

23 TUESDAY   *Moon Age Day 23   Moon Sign Cancer*

am . . . .

pm . . . .
As the lunar low retreats so you could find some unexpected and perhaps
confusing issues beginning to surface. Think about these carefully but
not for too long. If demands are being made on your time, it might be
all you can do to keep up. There isn't much time to stand and stare – at
least not until later in the day.

24 WEDNESDAY   *Moon Age Day 24   Moon Sign Cancer*

am . . . .

pm . . . .
Energy levels are enhanced, as is popularity and your ability to get others
to do your bidding. The Archer should be right back in gear and able to
manipulate almost any situation. This doesn't mean you should put
yourself in charge of everything because you can still run out of steam in
a physical sense. Be selective and pace yourself.

25 THURSDAY   ☿   *Moon Age Day 25   Moon Sign Leo*

am . . . .

pm . . . .
Trends now assist you to get the very best from romantic attachments
and from all forms of relationship that have no professional connection.
Work matters may be slightly less secure, and you could decide to allow
colleagues to make the running. The fact is that you are somewhat less
interested in succeeding for now.

26 FRIDAY   ☿   *Moon Age Day 26   Moon Sign Leo*

am . . . .

pm . . . .
If it seems as though your influence over certain aspects of life is slightly
lacking at present, this might be because you remain fairly uninterested in
getting ahead. This is unusual for Sagittarius and turns out to be nothing
more than a very temporary state of affairs. Your social and personal life
looks much better and has the power to hold your concentration.

27 SATURDAY   ☿   *Moon Age Day 27   Moon Sign Virgo*

am . . . .

pm . . . .
Your best response to any unexpected delays is to deal with them one at
a time and without undue panic. You can respond well to any sort of
demand that is made of you at the present time but should remain quite
aware that the weekend offers social and personal possibilities. Keep your
mind well balanced and fairly serene.

28 SUNDAY   ☿   *Moon Age Day 28   Moon Sign Virgo*

am . . . .

pm . . . .
You can make this a productive day as far as teamwork is concerned,
which is why sporting Archers should have such a good Sunday.
Co-operation with family members is also noteworthy and you seem to
have what it takes to convince others that you know what you are talking
about – even on those occasions when you don't!

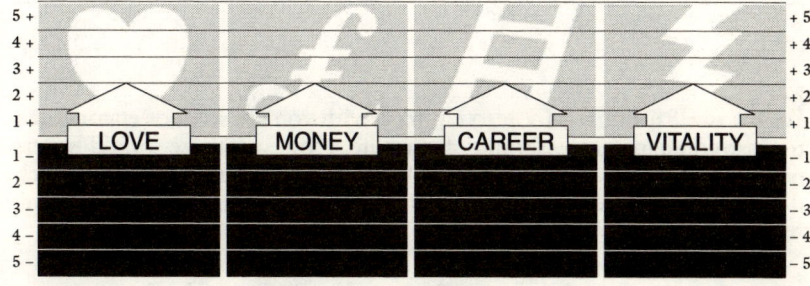

29 MONDAY ☿ *Moon Age Day 29   Moon Sign Libra*

am . . . .

pm . . . .
The present position of Mars encourages a slightly more cautious approach to what you take on today. Remember that your strengths are somewhat limited and that there will be times when you simply have to rely on the good offices and kindness of those around you. You can improve things later in the week.

30 TUESDAY ☿ *Moon Age Day 0   Moon Sign Libra*

am . . . .

pm . . . .
Your attitude at the moment is noteworthy and the only thing that is missing is that element of good luck that you can usually use. As a result you might have to work harder to get what you want and may also find obstacles being thrown in your path. Fortunately social and romantic trends are better for most of this week.

1 WEDNESDAY ☿ *Moon Age Day 1   Moon Sign Libra*

am . . . .

pm . . . .
Your competence is now enhanced and you can use it to deal with specific issues. Even if you are by no means at your noisiest or most progressive you have a strong sense of purpose and a desire to get on with things. Creative potential is well accented by the latter part of the day.

2 THURSDAY ☿ *Moon Age Day 2   Moon Sign Scorpio*

am . . . .

pm . . . .
With a twelfth-house Moon to contend with you are still not encouraged to push too hard in any sphere of your life. However, there should be less frustration now because you probably don't care about getting too much done. If ever there was a period of the year to sit back and watch life happening around you, this is it.

3 FRIDAY ☿ *Moon Age Day 3* *Moon Sign Scorpio*

am . . . .

pm . . . .
Even if you are still quite lethargic in some ways, you can get yourself in the right frame of mind to do some planning. Avoid major decisions until tomorrow because the lunar high is on the way. The end of a fairly negative and even frustrating period is in sight and you only have to wait a few more hours to get back on form.

4 SATURDAY ☿ *Moon Age Day 4* *Moon Sign Sagittarius*

am . . . .

pm . . . .
You can make this one of the best days of October, and even though the arrival of the weekend might prevent you from doing very much in a professional sense, you could still be champing at the bit in other ways. There's no such thing as a sense of proportion for Sagittarius today, and you may decide you want everything – all at once.

5 SUNDAY ☿ *Moon Age Day 5* *Moon Sign Sagittarius*

am . . . .

pm . . . .
You can now get a great deal done and as well as achieving your own objectives you can help others to do the same. Why not spend some time with your partner or lover and make it plain just how important they are to you? When it comes to dreaming up inspirational social activities you can be top of the tree during this particular Sunday.

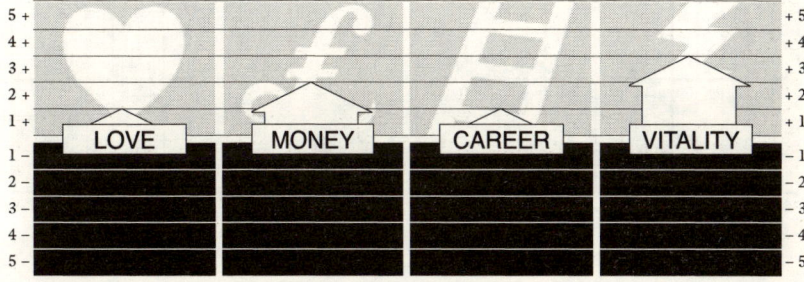

October 2008

YOUR MONTH AT A GLANCE

$\oplus$ = Opportunities are around $\ominus$ = Be on the defensive   ◯ = Life is pretty ordinary

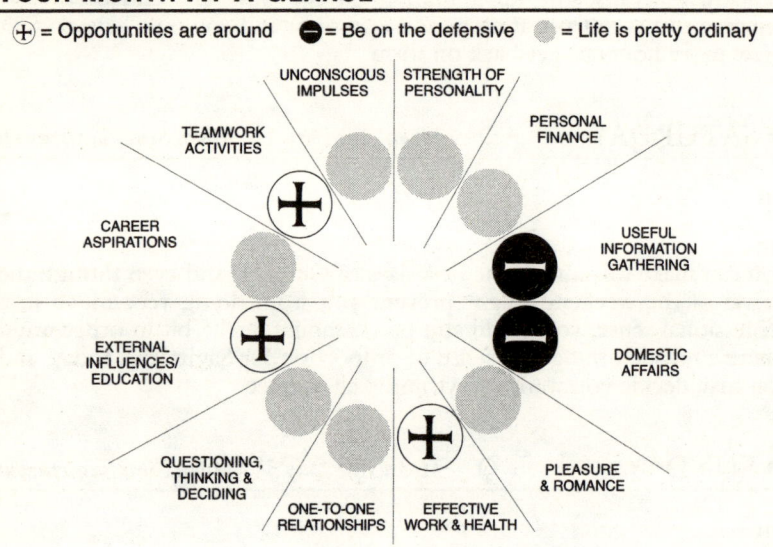

OCTOBER HIGHS AND LOWS

Here I show you how the rhythms of the Moon will affect you this month. Like the tide, your energies and abilities will rise and fall with its pattern. When it is above the centre line, go for it, when it is below, you should be resting.

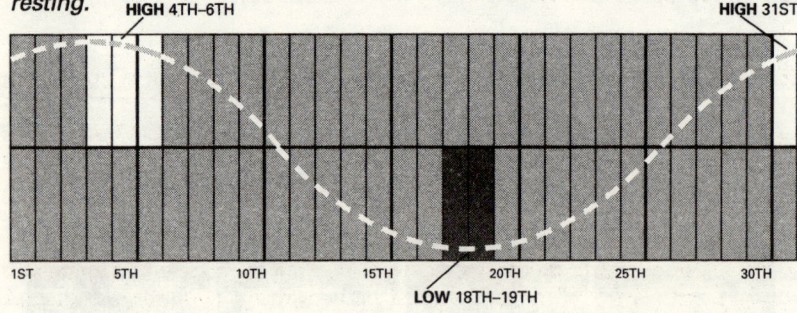

6 MONDAY   ☿   *Moon Age Day 6   Moon Sign Sagittarius*

am . . . .

pm . . . .
By all means share interesting ideas with others today, but when it comes
to getting things done you would be better off relying on your own
initiative. This is because those around you, no matter how willing they
may be, will not arrange things the way you want, and may not have your
staying power either.

7 TUESDAY   ☿   *Moon Age Day 7   Moon Sign Capricorn*

am . . . .

pm . . . .
You can get closer to some of your goals at the moment using a
combination of sound common sense and raw intuition. This is a strange
concoction and one that anyone other than another Sagittarian would
find difficult to understand. Energy levels remain generally high and
there isn't much you need to shy away from now.

8 WEDNESDAY   ☿   *Moon Age Day 8   Moon Sign Capricorn*

am . . . .

pm . . . .
If life is fairly chaotic at present, it might seem as though you are either
shirking or sidelining some of your responsibilities. Even if you don't
actually have enough time to get everything done you need to reassure
those around you that it is your intention to get round to all your duties
as soon as it becomes possible.

9 THURSDAY   ☿   *Moon Age Day 9   Moon Sign Aquarius*

am . . . .

pm . . . .
Don't be too quick to take offence today because there may be some
people around who seem to insult you at every turn. In fact, most
individuals are trying to offer you support but you just can't appreciate
the fact right now. All of this should become plain with the passing of
time and what is required today is extra patience.

10 FRIDAY
☿ *Moon Age Day 10* *Moon Sign Aquarius*

am . . . .

pm . . . .
Your normal work routines may now be interrupted by various small mishaps, meaning that some tasks have to be undertaken again. Don't give in to doubts or worries that are not based in reality, and do your best to stay optimistic. This might not be very easy, but at least you can keep life interesting and, on occasions, very funny.

11 SATURDAY
☿ *Moon Age Day 11* *Moon Sign Aquarius*

am . . . .

pm . . . .
You may now decide that ambitious projects will have to be put on hold, in favour or simply doing what you expect of yourself and what others are anxious for you to do. Your sense of fulfilment is closely tied to personal attachments at the present time, and your ego can be slightly dented if someone very important to you lets you down.

12 SUNDAY
☿ *Moon Age Day 12* *Moon Sign Pisces*

am . . . .

pm . . . .
The focus is now on activities that take place behind closed doors, particularly if you are not all that keen to get out and about as much as is usually the case for the Archer. Chances are that you will be fairly content with your own company and that you won't be seeking too much in the way of society.

	LOVE	MONEY	CAREER	VITALITY
5 +				+ 5
4 +				+ 4
3 +				+ 3
2 +				+ 2
1 +				+ 1
1 -				- 1
2 -				- 2
3 -				- 3
4 -				- 4
5 -				- 5

13 MONDAY ☿ *Moon Age Day 13   Moon Sign Pisces*

am . . . .

pm . . . .
There is just a slight possibility that you could be allowing hunches to gain the upper hand and as a result you could be involving yourself in something that is just a little dodgy. You really do need to know what you are doing at the present time, because although success is never far from you, scrupulous honesty is essential.

14 TUESDAY ☿ *Moon Age Day 14   Moon Sign Aries*

am . . . .

pm . . . .
You can now get things more or less back to normal now that planetary trends are settling down for you. Today should offer more in the way of confidence and certainty, whilst you can seek out support from those around you. Most important of all is the fact that your confidence returns.

15 WEDNESDAY ☿ *Moon Age Day 15   Moon Sign Aries*

am . . . .

pm . . . .
Although you still need to pace yourself it should be possible to get through more or less everything that is really important today. At the same time your social impulses are enhanced again and you may not be at all content if you are expected to keep your head down all that time. Mixing with others can work wonders.

16 THURSDAY ☿ *Moon Age Day 16   Moon Sign Taurus*

am . . . .

pm . . . .
You would still be wise to stay away from high-risk situations, at least until well after the coming weekend. It's worth keeping all your dealings transparent and above-board to such an extent that nobody could accuse you of doing anything shady. The more you explain yourself today, the greater will be the useful support that you can gain.

17 FRIDAY

Moon Age Day 17   Moon Sign Taurus

am . . . .

pm . . . .
You can afford to show great sympathy at the moment for anyone who is
having problems or who cannot deal with situations without becoming
deeply anxious. Not only can you offer advice but you also have what it
takes to assume command and to sort things out. This ability gets you
noticed and means you will have the support you need later.

18 SATURDAY

Moon Age Day 18   Moon Sign Gemini

am . . . .

pm . . . .
Personal and intimate matters bring out the best in you today and it's just
as well they do because the lunar low isn't an ideal time to get anything
concrete done. Take time out to show your lover just how important they
are to you, and do what you can to drive away your own blues.

19 SUNDAY

Moon Age Day 19   Moon Sign Gemini

am . . . .

pm . . . .
Practical matters are still not favoured, and some of your dreams and
ambitions might seem to be either in tatters or at the very least becoming
less likely by the moment. That's probably because you are showing the
pessimistic side of your nature. Be prepared simply to watch and wait
rather than taking drastic action.

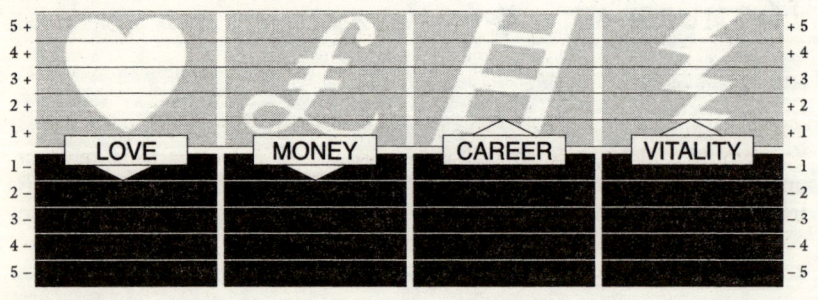

20 MONDAY
Moon Age Day 20   Moon Sign Cancer

am . . . .

pm . . . .
You can improve things noticeably as today wears on and you have a chance to get back on track with regard to some of your longed-for eventualities. Now you can't leave things open to chance but need to put in that extra bit of effort that can make all the difference. You may decide to seek help from friends.

21 TUESDAY
Moon Age Day 21   Moon Sign Cancer

am . . . .

pm . . . .
Trends suggest a vulnerability to the tactics of dishonest people. Keep your ears and eyes open and turn your intuition up to full when it comes to assessing those around you. Not everyone has your best interests at heart, and when it comes right down to it you have to be fully conversant with all that is happening.

22 WEDNESDAY
Moon Age Day 22   Moon Sign Leo

am . . . .

pm . . . .
You can make the most of positive career influences now, and might even steal a march on the opposition. Fortunately you can afford to worry less right now about the details of life and should be taking more notice of the personal and social possibilities that are available.

23 THURSDAY
Moon Age Day 23   Moon Sign Leo

am . . . .

pm . . . .
There is plenty of reason to be out of bed early today and getting on quickly with all jobs that need to be done as a matter of routine. This should allow you more hours later to do whatever takes your fancy. This would be a good day for travel and for getting out and about generally. You need to see new faces and places.

24 FRIDAY

Moon Age Day 24   Moon Sign Virgo

am . . . .

pm . . . .
What you hear from others could turn out to be extremely helpful today
and could help you to move much closer to something very important in
a professional sense. Away from work you have what it takes to turn
heads and to be much more positive in your general attitude than has
been the case for quite some time. Be prepared to shine.

25 SATURDAY

Moon Age Day 25   Moon Sign Virgo

am . . . .

pm . . . .
Mars is now in your solar twelfth house, moving the focus away from
your forceful and dominant side and towards your receptive, kind and
helpful nature. The only slight setback with Mars in this position is that
you are not quite as ready as you would sometimes be when it comes to
defending your opinions.

26 SUNDAY

Moon Age Day 26   Moon Sign Virgo

am . . . .

pm . . . .
You can't afford to trust to luck as much as you sometimes would and
need to check and recheck details whenever possible. Today offers scope
to move closer to your heart's desire in a personal sense and can offer
much in the way of social diversions. What it won't do is to make you a
great deal better off financially.

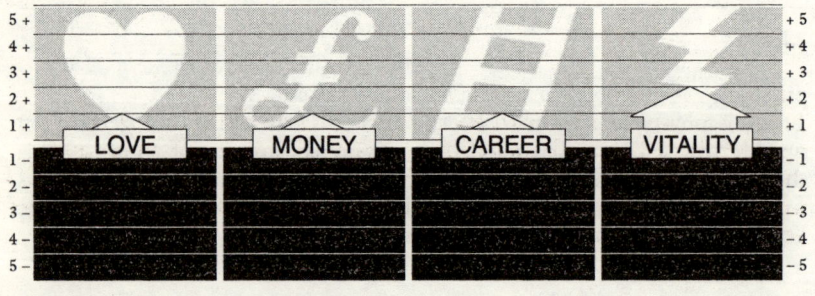

27 MONDAY
Moon Age Day 27   Moon Sign Libra

am . . . .

pm . . . .
With the Sun now in your solar twelfth house you can be thoughtful, considerate and quieter than might sometimes be the case, but this needn't prevent you from getting on well in a general sense. The start of a new week is a chance to achieve more of what you want at work, though possibly not in quite the way you would actually expect.

28 TUESDAY
Moon Age Day 28   Moon Sign Libra

am . . . .

pm . . . .
Any slight anxieties now can best be alleviated by sharing your worries with others. You can persuade someone in your vicinity to listen to what you have to say and offer advice. You are also presently very supportive of younger or vulnerable family members.

29 WEDNESDAY
Moon Age Day 0   Moon Sign Scorpio

am . . . .

pm . . . .
Trends now encourage the Archer to act on instinct, which is fine just as long as you let others know that this is the case. The only difficulty today comes if you keep quiet and simply do your own thing. This can lead to others feeling isolated, in which case they could respond in a fairly aggressive or untypical manner.

30 THURSDAY
Moon Age Day 1   Moon Sign Scorpio

am . . . .

pm . . . .
It shouldn't be long before you can get life to turn out more the way you would wish, and for the moment you need to clear the decks for action. A day to get all unfinished jobs out of the way and be bold in your forward planning. New social possibilities are available, with sporting activities being favoured for quite a few Archers now.

31 FRIDAY
Moon Age Day 2   Moon Sign Sagittarius

am . . . .

pm . . . .

The lunar high comes along and brings with it the necessary breeze of change that can blow away some of the recent difficulties. Today works best if you are determined, happy to go that extra mile and willing to do whatever is necessary in terms of changing old or outmoded routines. It's worth getting to grips with your finances.

1 SATURDAY
Moon Age Day 3   Moon Sign Sagittarius

am . . . .

pm . . . .

Put your creative energy where it matters the most and don't be at all shy about showing the world at large what you are capable of doing. If others make a fuss of you it is certain they are doing so because they really rate you, and as a result you can afford to bask in their respect and admiration. Forget any sense of proportion for now.

2 SUNDAY
Moon Age Day 4   Moon Sign Sagittarius

am . . . .

pm . . . .

Your affable nature is what matters the most right now and this is a Sunday during which you can shine in any social setting. Rather than sitting around at home, why not get out into the wider world, showing everyone just how positive and aspiring the Archer is? Put minor worries to the back of your mind or, better still, sort them out.

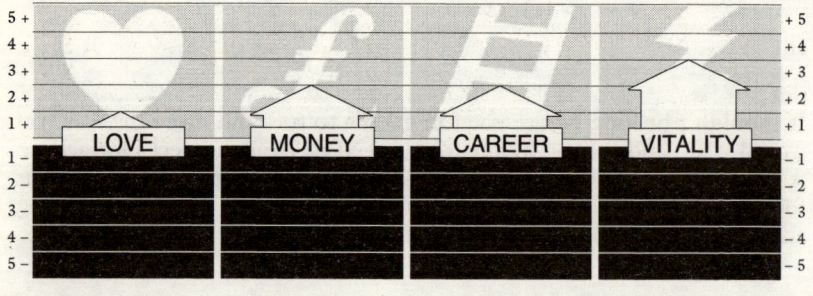

November
2008

YOUR MONTH AT A GLANCE

⊕ = Opportunities are around   ⊖ = Be on the defensive   ⬤ = Life is pretty ordinary

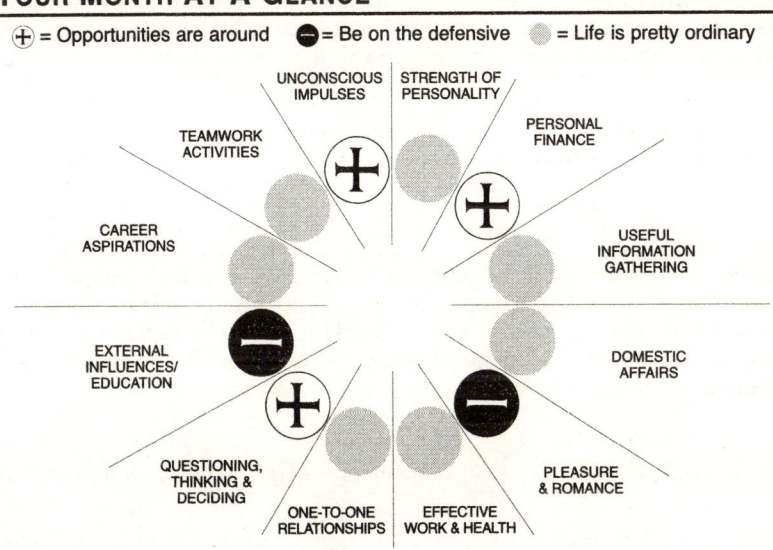

NOVEMBER HIGHS AND LOWS

Here I show you how the rhythms of the Moon will affect you this month. Like the tide, your energies and abilities will rise and fall with its pattern. When it is above the centre line, go for it, when it is below, you should be resting. **HIGH** 1ST–2ND   **HIGH** 28TH–29TH

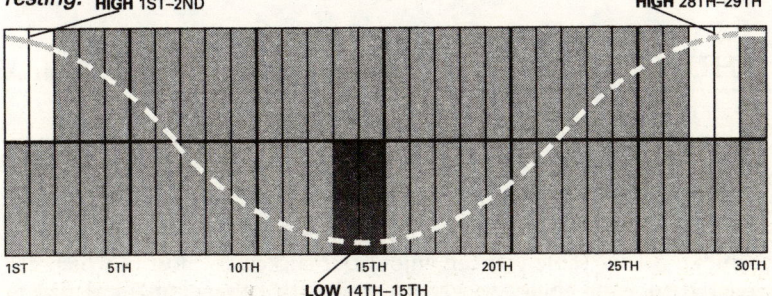

1ST   5TH   10TH   15TH   20TH   25TH   30TH

LOW 14TH–15TH

3 MONDAY   *Moon Age Day 5   Moon Sign Capricorn*

am . . . .

pm . . . .
Any chance to strike up some form of new social contract should be grasped with both hands. This is particularly the case when you are dealing with unconventional types, many of whom seem to be especially attractive to you at this time. By all means have fun when you are away from work and socialise as much as possible in November.

4 TUESDAY   *Moon Age Day 6   Moon Sign Capricorn*

am . . . .

pm . . . .
Today can be especially helpful day in terms of communication. Your ability to get the message across to others is enhanced, and you shouldn't miss a single minute when it comes to telling it how it is. Some practical jobs could be a chore, but not if you get them out of the way very early in the day.

5 WEDNESDAY   *Moon Age Day 7   Moon Sign Aquarius*

am . . . .

pm . . . .
You can get the best of both worlds today when it comes to work and home, and it should also be quite possible for you to mix business with pleasure in a very successful way. It appears that the Archer is truly on form at this time, especially when it comes to getting your ideas and opinions across to all sorts of people.

6 THURSDAY   *Moon Age Day 8   Moon Sign Aquarius*

am . . . .

pm . . . .
The Sun remains in your solar twelfth house until much later this month, doing little to help you to surge ahead as much as will be the case in December. All the same you can enjoy your successes, most of which will be related to your ability to get on well with others. An ideal day to contact people at a distance.

7 FRIDAY
Moon Age Day 9   Moon Sign Aquarius

am . . . .

pm . . . .
Everyday events come and go, and you may be able to get a great deal done whilst in a state of automatic pilot. If your mind is often elsewhere, there could be a sort of dreamy quality to your nature that others find distinctly appealing. Don't be at all surprised if you find that you can become someone's romantic ideal.

8 SATURDAY
Moon Age Day 10   Moon Sign Pisces

am . . . .

pm . . . .
The time is right to look at finances and the many ways you can improve them in the days and weeks ahead. It could be that there is slightly more money around than you might have expected or it is possible that you are simply being much more careful in the way you use cash that you have. It's worth keeping lists just now.

9 SUNDAY
Moon Age Day 11   Moon Sign Pisces

am . . . .

pm . . . .
Mars is moving onwards in your solar chart and is gradually approaching your solar first house. For the moment however it remains in your twelfth house, from where it can encourage you to simmer inside over something you see as being an injustice. This is to be avoided, and it would be far better to tell people how you feel.

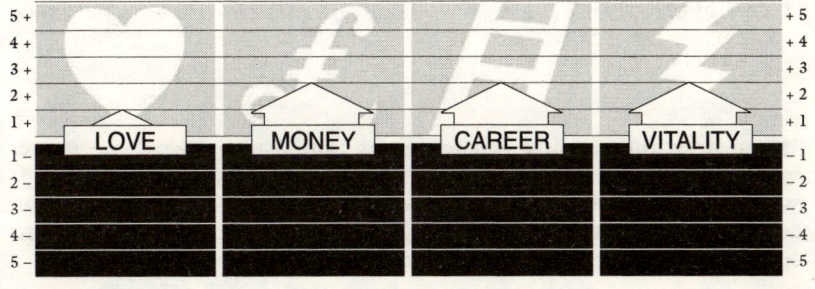

10 MONDAY
Moon Age Day 12   Moon Sign Aries

am . . . .

pm . . . .
If others are especially demanding today, much of your time may be given over to sorting them out in one way or another. This trend is so evident that it might be quite difficult to get anything much done for yourself – which could lead to some frustration. In a social sense you can now afford to ring the changes regularly.

11 TUESDAY
Moon Age Day 13   Moon Sign Aries

am . . . .

pm . . . .
This is one of the best days of the month during which to get new projects off the ground and to use your know-how when it matters the most. Not that you are capable of doing absolutely everything. There may be moments when it would be best to call in the support of an expert – even though you may resent doing so.

12 WEDNESDAY
Moon Age Day 14   Moon Sign Taurus

am . . . .

pm . . . .
Your strength lies in remaining one of the main attractions in your social circle and finding the means to mix business with pleasure in a very useful and enjoyable way. Take over some of the organisation if you want things to go seamlessly, otherwise you could discover that details are either forgotten or mishandled.

13 THURSDAY
Moon Age Day 15   Moon Sign Taurus

am . . . .

pm . . . .
If you insist on asserting your opinions and having your say no matter what, you could fall foul of someone who has very different ideas. It would be far better at the moment to agree with people rather than arguing. All the same, you won't be crossed and will cut off your nose to spite your face under certain circumstances.

14 FRIDAY   *Moon Age Day 16   Moon Sign Gemini*

am . . . .

pm . . . .
Whilst it is possible that you are presently eager for success, you might have to work that much harder to achieve it. Although not really a stumbling block to you, it is just possible that you may look with envy at certain individuals who seem to come up smelling of roses, no matter how little effort they put in at present.

15 SATURDAY   *Moon Age Day 17   Moon Sign Gemini*

am . . . .

pm . . . .
The lunar low is still around and you might have to work that much harder to achieve your objectives – even if it would be more sensible simply to put things on hold for a day or two. You remain quite adamant about your own opinions and won't let anyone tell you that you are wrong. Keep up your efforts to make changes at home.

16 SUNDAY   *Moon Age Day 18   Moon Sign Cancer*

am . . . .

pm . . . .
Energy is back after the lunar low, and you can begin to make plans for a busy time ahead. The fact that the cold weather is returning is unlikely to inspire you, but with thoughts of home and family in your mind at present the contemplation of nights by the fireside might seem quite inspiring.

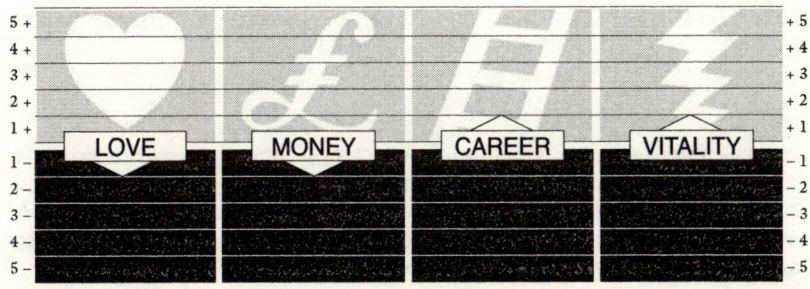

17 MONDAY   *Moon Age Day 19   Moon Sign Cancer*

am . . . .

pm . . . .
Make the most of any favours that others do for you today. This could be
because you are smiling so much and putting yourself out on their behalf
without even realising the fact. Gains coming from the direction of
simple good luck are also possible, together with meetings and
discussions that offer significant success.

18 TUESDAY   *Moon Age Day 20   Moon Sign Leo*

am . . . .

pm . . . .
At least you can get plenty of folks on your side today. Moving away from
the misunderstandings that might have been present fairly recently, you
are now in a position to take the line of least resistance and to avoid
complications as a result. In the end this could be a somewhat quieter day
but one that carries its own rewards.

19 WEDNESDAY   *Moon Age Day 21   Moon Sign Leo*

am . . . .

pm . . . .
If things mechanical are giving you problems right now, it might be best
to leave them to people who know what they are doing. Typical
Sagittarian tampering might only make matters worse, though it is just
possible that you will learn something on the way. Try not to annoy
friends today.

20 THURSDAY   *Moon Age Day 22   Moon Sign Leo*

am . . . .

pm . . . .
A potentially busy day which might put you under some sort of pressure
at a time when you would prefer things to go smoothly. Appointments
could be delayed or even cancelled and it may seem difficult to get truly
in touch with people you know are going to be important to you. Keep
a sense of proportion with family members.

21 FRIDAY
Moon Age Day 23   Moon Sign Virgo

am . . . .

pm . . . .
The Sun is about to enter your solar first house, offering you a very much more progressive period. You can use it to help things to go smoothly in a day-to-day sense, which definitely hasn't been the case throughout much of November so far. Get an early start today and tackle routines as early as you can.

22 SATURDAY
Moon Age Day 24   Moon Sign Virgo

am . . . .

pm . . . .
It's time to put yourself in the limelight and to work towards a weekend that can be very special to you and those you love. The Archer can afford to be quite romantic at present, and it looks as though you can make the best of impressions on someone who is truly important to you. Stand by to meet Sagittarius the lover – an inspiring sight!

23 SUNDAY
Moon Age Day 25   Moon Sign Libra

am . . . .

pm . . . .
Trends assist you to remain on fine form and to do whatever is necessary to make the sort of impression for which the Archer is famous. People like you for your dynamism, your sense of humour and your easy-going attitude, all of which are present in great measure. Don't rely on too much financial support for the moment.

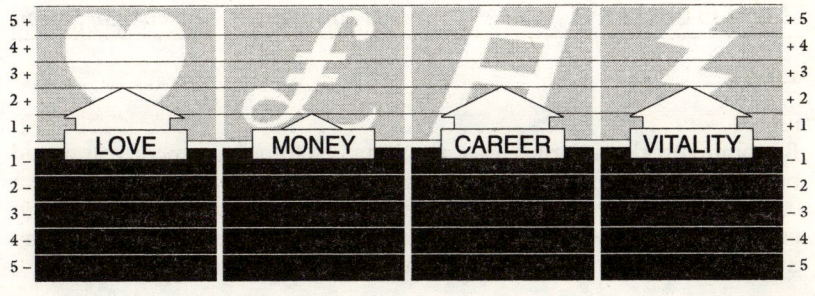

24 MONDAY
Moon Age Day 26   Moon Sign Libra

am . . . .

pm . . . .
When it comes to new and fascinating enterprises you can be second to none at this time. That first-house Sun offers new incentives and gives you a golden touch in terms of your business acumen. Nothing need prevent you from acting on impulse most of the time, but that's when you tend to be at your best and when you can make life go your way.

25 TUESDAY
Moon Age Day 27   Moon Sign Scorpio

am . . . .

pm . . . .
If you quieten things down just a little for a couple of days, this will at least give you the chance to retrench and to think again about certain matters. You shouldn't feel as though life is squashing you in any way, because despite the present of a twelfth-house Moon you 'seem' to be in charge, and that is what matters the most to the Archer.

26 WEDNESDAY
Moon Age Day 28   Moon Sign Scorpio

am . . . .

pm . . . .
Conforming to the expectations that others have of you has rarely been easier than it will be today, particularly if you are now far less determined to get your own way. Not that anyone will be pulling the wool over your eyes. You know very well what you want but can be a great deal more circumspect in the way you do things.

27 THURSDAY
Moon Age Day 29   Moon Sign Scorpio

am . . . .

pm . . . .
By tomorrow the lunar high comes along but for the moment you would be wise to pause and take stock. Don't rush anything but watch and wait until you know the time is right. If ever there was a time to sort out your preferences and wishes this is that time, and you should have little or no difficulty in showing friends how important they are to you.

28 FRIDAY
Moon Age Day 0   Moon Sign Sagittarius

am . . . .

pm . . . .
Pushing ahead and getting what you want from life are simply two of your talents right now. Energy is definitely enhanced, supporting activities at work or in terms of your major responsibilities. There are gains to be made by simply being in the right place at the best time, and you have a great desire to prosper.

29 SATURDAY
Moon Age Day 1   Moon Sign Sagittarius

am . . . .

pm . . . .
With the lunar high comes a definite sense of drive and enthusiasm. You shouldn't find it at all hard to ring the changes and you might even decide to spend time away from home. Despite these facts, and the lunar high, you can also afford to spend time with someone you know well and to share moments with them.

30 SUNDAY
Moon Age Day 2   Moon Sign Capricorn

am . . . .

pm . . . .
You can make the last day of the month settled, contented and generally happy. It might not bring you quite the benefits of the last couple of days, but if you need to sort out certain aspects of your life you will be in the best frame of mind to do so. It isn't your starts that are potentially problematic at the moment, but rather your finishes!

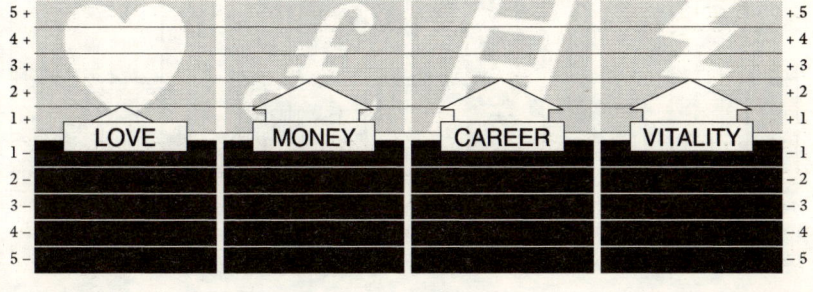

December 2008

YOUR MONTH AT A GLANCE

⊕ = Opportunities are around ⊖ = Be on the defensive ⬤ = Life is pretty ordinary

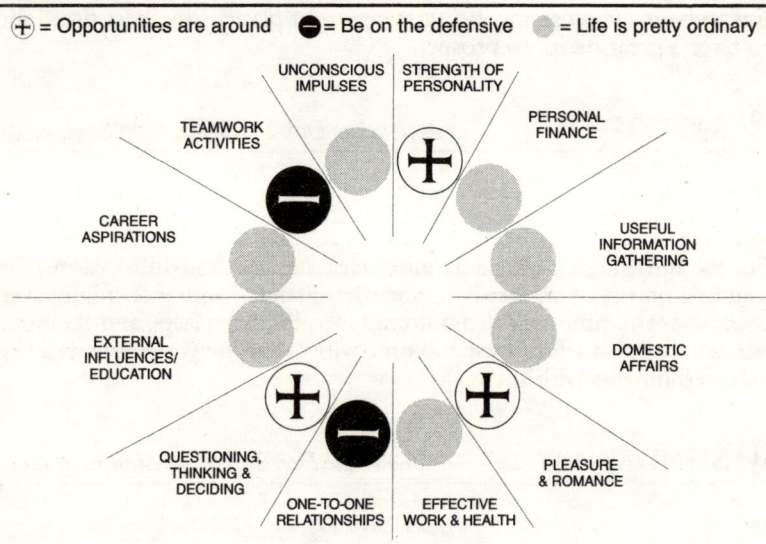

DECEMBER HIGHS AND LOWS

Here I show you how the rhythms of the Moon will affect you this month. Like the tide, your energies and abilities will rise and fall with its pattern. When it is above the centre line, go for it, when it is below, you should be resting.

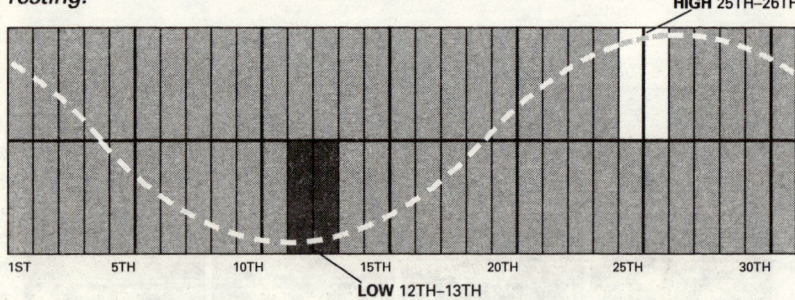

HIGH 25TH–26TH

LOW 12TH–13TH

148

1 MONDAY   *Moon Age Day 3   Moon Sign Capricorn*

am . . . .

pm . . . .
Some of your plans may be up in the air at the moment but if you stop still for a while and think about things, you have scope to get on better in the longer term. Why not find something to take your mind off small worries, most of which are worth nothing? One option is to seek support and entertainment from friends.

2 TUESDAY   *Moon Age Day 4   Moon Sign Capricorn*

am . . . .

pm . . . .
Today would be a good time to review your innermost thoughts, especially in terms of personal attachments and what you want from them now and for the future. Close family ties are emphasised at present – probably more so than would normally be the case. Financial advantages are there for the taking.

3 WEDNESDAY   *Moon Age Day 5   Moon Sign Aquarius*

am . . . .

pm . . . .
As far as your work is concerned the high-energy phase offered by the Sun in your solar first house should be continuing. If you know what you want at the moment, you needn't be tardy about going out to get it. This could also be a fairly quirky period with some strange happenings – most of which you can turn to your advantage.

4 THURSDAY   *Moon Age Day 6   Moon Sign Aquarius*

am . . . .

pm . . . .
Personal communications are well starred for the moment, assisting you to get on especially well with like-minded people. You may find yourself attracted to other Sagittarians or to people born under the zodiac signs of Aries and Leo. The people you may not get on with at the moment are those who refuse to try anything.

5 FRIDAY

Moon Age Day 7   Moon Sign Pisces

am . . . .

pm . . . .
Even if there are financial obligations to be dealt with now and across the weekend, you have what it takes to sort things out in a cheerful and successful way. You can best avoid confusion in the family by making sure that everyone knows exactly what is expected of them – and when. There could well be some very amusing moments today.

6 SATURDAY

Moon Age Day 8   Moon Sign Pisces

am . . . .

pm . . . .
If you turn your mind towards romance this weekend, you are unlikely to be disappointed. Relationships can work out especially well for you under present planetary trends, and you may even decide to sweep someone off their feet. Whether this is the right person or not remains to be seen.

7 SUNDAY

Moon Age Day 9   Moon Sign Pisces

am . . . .

pm . . . .
A wonderful time is possible regarding home and family, and trends encourage you to spend more time with relatives than might normally be the case for the Archer. You get on especially well with younger people or those who have a very young attitude to life. Miserable types are best avoided today.

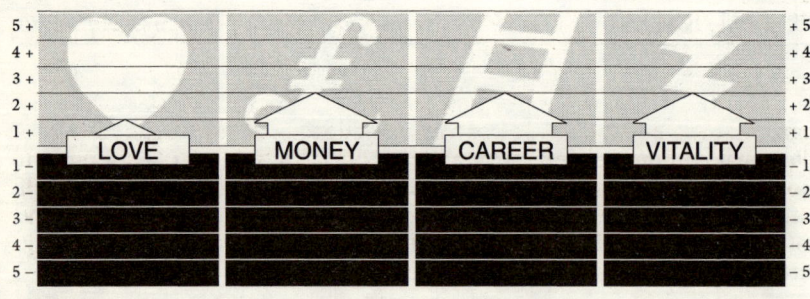

8 MONDAY   *Moon Age Day 10   Moon Sign Aries*

am . . . .

pm . . . .
Today would be a favourable time for communicating with others, for travelling or for simply chewing the fat. You might not get as much done as you would wish in a practical sense, but that won't really matter if you are enjoying yourself. Life can't be all work, and you function much better when you are happy.

9 TUESDAY   *Moon Age Day 11   Moon Sign Aries*

am . . . .

pm . . . .
The focus is now on people you don't see too often. The time is right to make contact, and welcome them back into your life. Nostalgia in a general sense plays a part in your life at the moment, so why not search out old school friends or long-lost lovers?

10 WEDNESDAY   *Moon Age Day 12   Moon Sign Taurus*

am . . . .

pm . . . .
For a couple of astrological reasons you may now decide to hold back on your feelings or to suppress something that really should be said. This won't do you any good at all because the Archer needs to speak out and you always feel better when you have. Finances could be stronger than of late, but you can make them even better soon.

11 THURSDAY   *Moon Age Day 13   Moon Sign Taurus*

am . . . .

pm . . . .
Joint financial matters could prompt a decision to change things at home or with your partner. This needs to be done as a result of discussions and is not something you should undertake alone. A cavalier attitude is not your best option for the moment, since it could lead to resentment or even arguments.

12 FRIDAY
Moon Age Day 14   Moon Sign Gemini

am . . . .

pm . . . .
The lunar low brings certain restrictions, and doesn't assist you to do exactly what you would wish in a social sense. It looks as though now and the first part of the weekend will bring greater responsibilities. Fatigue also has a part to play today.

13 SATURDAY
Moon Age Day 15   Moon Sign Gemini

am . . . .

pm . . . .
If there are obstacles about at the moment you will simply have to take these in your stride, rather than reacting to them in a way that brings problems into your life. A day's rest and relaxation won't do you any harm at all, except inside your head. By tomorrow you should be able to get yourself more or less back to normal.

14 SUNDAY
Moon Age Day 16   Moon Sign Cancer

am . . . .

pm . . . .
The more you are amongst familiar faces today, the better you are likely to feel. It may have occurred to you for the first time that Christmas is just around the corner, and today represents a period when you can come to terms with the fact. If the decorations are not up yet, this is an ideal time to get those boxes out.

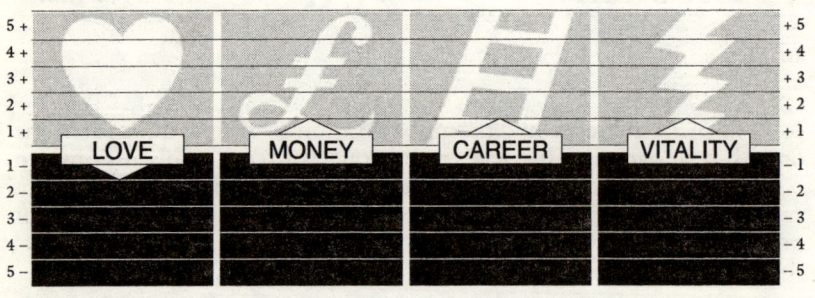

15 MONDAY   *Moon Age Day 17   Moon Sign Cancer*

am . . . .

pm . . . .
The general progress you always seek is on offer in great measure today, so much so that you might have difficulty keeping up with all the possibilities. Not only can you be very active in a professional sense, there are also social opportunities. After a blur of a day you may be quite happy to get to bed.

16 TUESDAY   *Moon Age Day 18   Moon Sign Leo*

am . . . .

pm . . . .
Your sense of freedom knows no bounds and the only slight fly in the ointment at the moment could be that you can't pursue everything you would wish. Is it because you are surrounded by people who can't or don't want to keep up? Be reasonable though, because not everyone has your level of determination or energy.

17 WEDNESDAY   *Moon Age Day 19   Moon Sign Leo*

am . . . .

pm . . . .
Teamwork issues are very favourably highlighted at present and you get on best when you co-operate. This isn't simply a matter that has a bearing on your life at work, but relates to your social life too. Christmas gatherings are starting and as usual Sagittarius has potential to be the life and soul of the party – or many parties!

18 THURSDAY   *Moon Age Day 20   Moon Sign Virgo*

am . . . .

pm . . . .
Your strength lies in your wish to build a caring environment in which everyone will be happy. That's fine just as long as people want to join in, but your own particular brand of utopia might not appeal to everyone. It may be a matter of using a little psychology if you really want to get things moving.

19 FRIDAY
Moon Age Day 21   Moon Sign Virgo

am . . . .

pm . . . .
If you want to get your own way in practical matters, you may not be especially happy if this proves impossible to achieve. A little patience is required and that is a commodity that can be sadly lacking for the Archer. When things are not going your way you need to turn your mind to other matters and to try something different.

20 SATURDAY
Moon Age Day 22   Moon Sign Libra

am . . . .

pm . . . .
You could benefit somewhat from being on your own a little this Saturday, or at least by being in the company of people with whom you don't have to try very hard. It's a fact that the Archer is always on duty when it comes to making a good impression, and there are times when this can become quite wearing. Why not simply be yourself today?

21 SUNDAY
Moon Age Day 23   Moon Sign Libra

am . . . .

pm . . . .
You can put your great versatility to good use today, perhaps by trying to be in a dozen different places at the same time. Somehow you could manage to achieve all that is expected of you, but it might be a tight squeeze on occasions. Maybe it might be best to restrict your actions a little, but of course that isn't really you, is it?

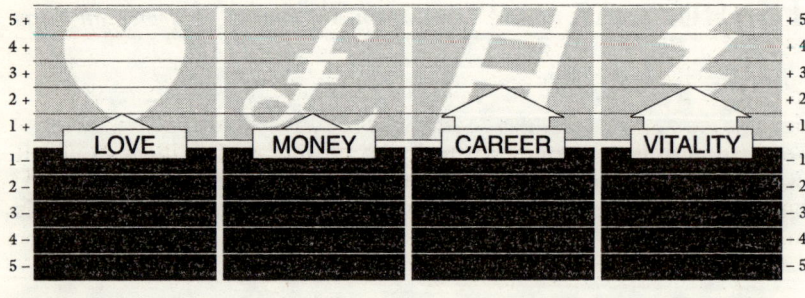

22 MONDAY
Moon Age Day 24   Moon Sign Scorpio

am . . . .

pm . . . .
Although you can make the most of a couple of quieter days as the Moon
passes through your solar twelfth house, you may decide to battle on
regardless of the planetary trends. At least if you exhaust yourself you will
know why, and then you have scope to take a few hours out.

23 TUESDAY
Moon Age Day 25   Moon Sign Scorpio

am . . . .

pm . . . .
There are conflicting interests about at the moment. On the one hand
there is a dreamy, nostalgic influence, but on the other there are strong
social demands coming in from so many different directions. Stagger
through today as best you can because tomorrow offers positive trends
and greater resilience.

24 WEDNESDAY
Moon Age Day 26   Moon Sign Scorpio

am . . . .

pm . . . .
Today offers a chance to catch up with things and get those last-minute
details sorted out ahead of Christmas itself. You might be having just a
little trouble with family members, some of whom seem to be getting
themselves into a stew about nothing at all. Having a chat with them can
work wonders.

25 THURSDAY
Moon Age Day 27   Moon Sign Sagittarius

am . . . .

pm . . . .
Christmas Day this year coincides with the lunar high as far as you are
concerned so you can make it a fast and furious sort of day, with plenty
to set it apart. You like things to be memorable and just now you should
be doing all you can to make certain this is the case. Capitalise on some
memorable surprises!

26 FRIDAY   *Moon Age Day 28   Moon Sign Sagittarius*

am . . . .

pm . . . .

How very good you are at bringing out the best in everyone. When things need organising you can be on hand to do it and there is unlikely to be a single part of today that isn't special in one way or another. Good luck is there for the taking, and you can find love in many places. Some of it might be completely unbidden!

27 SATURDAY   *Moon Age Day 0   Moon Sign Capricorn*

am . . . .

pm . . . .

If you have good and inspiring things to say to everyone, you can really boost your overall popularity at this time. Active and enterprising, the only slight problem at the moment is that you can't turn all these positive trends to your professional advantage. Friends could be demanding, but in a very positive way.

28 SUNDAY   *Moon Age Day 1   Moon Sign Capricorn*

am . . . .

pm . . . .

Bringing matters out into the open is fine, though you would be wise to be slightly careful about what you are saying, and to whom. The fact is that you can be too outspoken for your own good on occasions and will get by a great deal better if you use tact and diplomacy. Under present trends that may not be very easy.

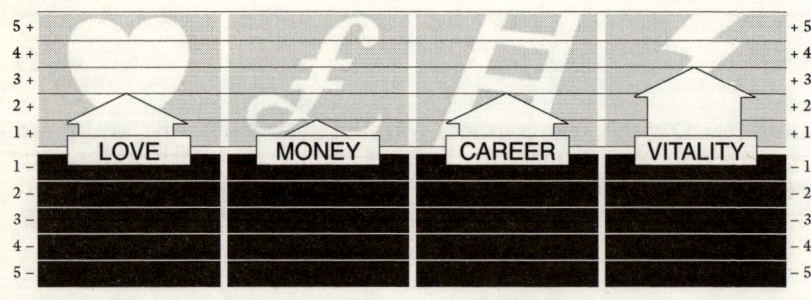

29 MONDAY   *Moon Age Day 2   Moon Sign Capricorn*

am . . . .

pm . . . .
It's worth taking the opportunity today to get a little more in the way of
relaxation than has been possible across the Christmas period as a whole.
There is nothing very quiet about your solar chart at the moment, so it
might be a case of enforcing some meditation. If you don't slow down
you could find some matters running out of control later.

30 TUESDAY   *Moon Age Day 3   Moon Sign Aquarius*

am . . . .

pm . . . .
Much of today has potential to be quite wonderful because your home
life in particular is well accented. Nostalgia returns but there is nothing
especially surprising about this for the Archer at this time of year. That's
fine just as long as you remember that the best place for you to be is not
in the past but rather contributing to the future.

31 WEDNESDAY   *Moon Age Day 4   Moon Sign Aquarius*

am . . . .

pm . . . .
The Sun is now in your solar second house and brings with it a slightly
more realistic attitude when it comes to your own capabilities. As a result
your view of the New Year should be sensible and well reasoned. By all
means get together with all your friends this evening, but paint the town
a slightly more muted shade of red than usual!

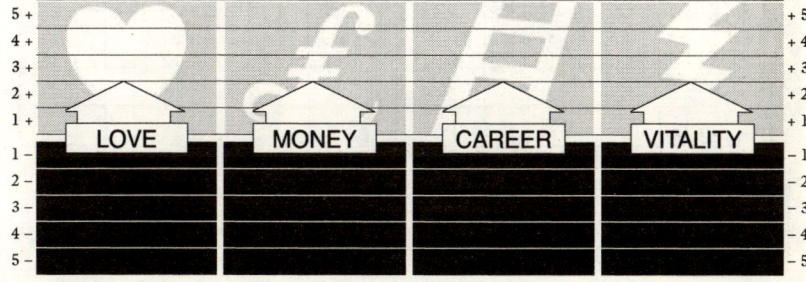

RISING SIGNS FOR SAGITTARIUS

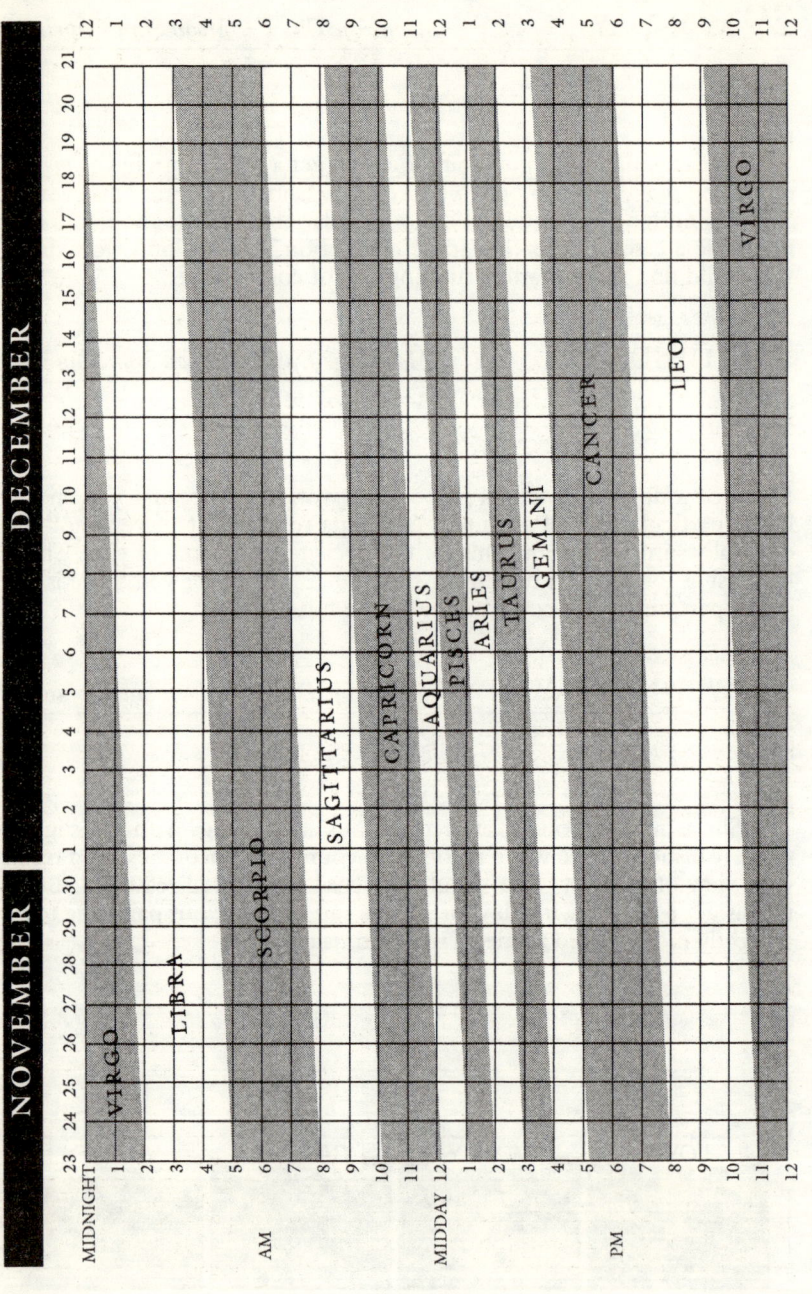

THE ZODIAC, PLANETS AND CORRESPONDENCES

The Earth revolves around the Sun once every calendar year, so when viewed from Earth the Sun appears in a different part of the sky as the year progresses. In astrology, these parts of the sky are divided into the signs of the zodiac and this means that the signs are organised in a circle. The circle begins with Aries and ends with Pisces.

Taking the zodiac sign as a starting point, astrologers then work with all the positions of planets, stars and many other factors to calculate horoscopes and birth charts and tell us what the stars have in store for us.

The table below shows the planets and Elements for each of the signs of the zodiac. Each sign belongs to one of the four Elements: Fire, Air, Earth or Water. Fire signs are creative and enthusiastic; Air signs are mentally active and thoughtful; Earth signs are constructive and practical; Water signs are emotional and have strong feelings.

It also shows the metals and gemstones associated with, or corresponding with, each sign. The correspondence is made when a metal or stone possesses properties that are held in common with a particular sign of the zodiac.

Finally, the table shows the opposite of each star sign – this is the opposite sign in the astrological circle.

Placed	Sign	Symbol	Element	Planet	Metal	Stone	Opposite
1	Aries	Ram	Fire	Mars	Iron	Bloodstone	Libra
2	Taurus	Bull	Earth	Venus	Copper	Sapphire	Scorpio
3	Gemini	Twins	Air	Mercury	Mercury	Tiger's Eye	Sagittarius
4	Cancer	Crab	Water	Moon	Silver	Pearl	Capricorn
5	Leo	Lion	Fire	Sun	Gold	Ruby	Aquarius
6	Virgo	Maiden	Earth	Mercury	Mercury	Sardonyx	Pisces
7	Libra	Scales	Air	Venus	Copper	Sapphire	Aries
8	Scorpio	Scorpion	Water	Pluto	Plutonium	Jasper	Taurus
9	Sagittarius	Archer	Fire	Jupiter	Tin	Topaz	Gemini
10	Capricorn	Goat	Earth	Saturn	Lead	Black Onyx	Cancer
11	Aquarius	Waterbearer	Air	Uranus	Uranium	Amethyst	Leo
12	Pisces	Fishes	Water	Neptune	Tin	Moonstone	Virgo